Reception Teacher Guide A

A Guide to Teaching for Mastery

Series Editor: Tony Staneff

Contents

Introduction and Meet the authors	page 4
What is *Power Maths*?	page 5
Your *Power Maths Reception* resources	page 6
Power Maths Reception, yearly overview	page 9
Teaching sequence	page 12
Day 1: Weekly starter	page 13
Day 2: Discover and Share	page 14
Day 3: Think together and Practice	page 15
Day 4: Challenge and Strengthen	page 16
Day 5: Practical activities and Reflect	page 17
Structures and representations	page 18
Applying the C-P-A approach in Reception	page 19
The *Power Maths* characters	page 20
Mathematical language	page 21
Keeping the class together	page 22
Variation helps visualisation	page 23

Unit 1 – Numbers to 5 — page 24
Week 1 – Counting to 1, 2 and 3	page 26
Week 2 – Counting to 4	page 32
Week 3 – Counting to 5	page 38

Unit 2 – Sorting — page 44
Week 4 – Sorting into 2 groups	page 46

Unit 3 – Comparing groups within 5 — page 52
Week 5 – Comparing quantities of identical objects	page 54
Week 6 – Comparing quantities of non-identical objects	page 60

Unit 4 – Change within 5 — page 66
Week 7 – One more	page 68
Week 8 – One less	page 74

Unit 5 – Time — page 80
Week 9 – My day	page 82

Unit 1 Observation sheet	page 88
Unit 2 Observation sheet	page 89
Unit 3 Observation sheet	page 90
Unit 4 Observation sheet	page 91
Unit 5 Observation sheet	page 92
Photocopiable 1: Number 0	page 93
Photocopiable 2: Number 1	page 94
Photocopiable 3: Number 2	page 95
Photocopiable 4: Number 3	page 96
Photocopiable 5: Number 4	page 97

Photocopiable 6: Number 5 — page 98
Photocopiable 7: Five frame — page 99
Photocopiable 8: Numbers to five — page 100
Photocopiable 9: Sequencing – Alex's Day — page 101

List of practical resources — page 102

Introduction

Foreword by the series editor and author, Tony Staneff

For far too long in the UK, maths has been feared by learners – and by many teachers, too. As a result, most learners consistently underachieve. More crucially, negative beliefs about ability, aptitude and the nature of maths are entrenched in children's thinking from an early age.

Yet, as someone who has loved maths all my life, I've always believed that every child has the capacity to succeed in maths. I've also had the great pleasure of leading teams and departments who share that belief and passion. Teaching for mastery, as practised in China and other South-East Asian jurisdictions since the 1980s, has confirmed my conviction that maths really is for everyone and not just those who have a special talent. In recent years, my team and I at Trinity Academy, Halifax, have had the privilege of researching with and working alongside some of the finest mastery practitioners from the UK and beyond, whose impact on learners' confidence, achievement and attitude is an inspiration.

The mastery approach recognises the value of developing the power to think rather than just do. It also recognises the value of making a coherent journey in which whole-class groups tackle concepts in very small steps, one by one. You cannot build securely on loose foundations – and it is just the same with maths: by creating a solid foundation of deep understanding, our children's skills and confidence will be strong and secure. What's more, the mindset of learner and teacher alike is fundamental: everyone can do maths … EVERYONE CAN!

I am proud to have been part of the extensive team responsible for turning the best of the world's practice, research, insights, and shared experiences into *Power Maths*, a unique teaching and learning resource developed especially for UK classrooms. *Power Maths* embodies our vision to help and support primary and Early Years teachers to transform every child's mathematical and personal development. 'Everyone can!' has become our mantra and our passion, and we hope it will be yours, too.

Now, explore and enjoy all the resources you need to teach for mastery, and please get back to us with your *Power Maths* experiences and stories!

Meet the authors

Tony Staneff, Series Editor

Vice Principal at Trinity Academy, Halifax, Tony also leads a team of mastery experts who help schools across the UK to develop teaching for mastery via nationally recognised CPD courses, problem-solving and reasoning resources, schemes of work, assessment materials and other tools.

 A team of experienced authors, including:

- **White Rose Maths** (Michael Gosling CEO, Tony Staneff, Beth Smith, Caroline Hamilton, Faye Hirst, Jane Brown and Amy How)

- **Beth Smith, Katie Williams, Faye Hirst and Caroline Hamilton** – Mastery Specialists with expertise in Early Years

 A group of teachers and maths co-ordinators

We have consulted our teacher group throughout the development of *Power Maths Reception* to ensure we are meeting their real needs in the classroom.

What is *Power Maths*?

Created especially for UK primary schools, and aligned with the National Curriculum and the Early Years Framework, *Power Maths* is a whole-class mastery resource that empowers every child to understand and succeed. *Power Maths* rejects the notion that some people simply 'can't do' maths. Instead, it develops growth mindsets and encourages hard work, practice and a willingness to see mistakes as learning tools.

Best practice consistently shows that mastery of small, cumulative steps builds a solid foundation of deep mathematical understanding. *Power Maths* combines interactive teaching tools, high-quality textbooks and continuing professional development (CPD) to help you equip children with a deep and long lasting understanding. Based on extensive evidence, and developed in partnership with practising teachers, *Power Maths* ensures that it meets the needs of children in the UK.

Power Maths and Mastery

Power Maths makes mastery practical and achievable by providing the structures, pathways, content, tools and support you need to make it happen in your classroom.

To develop mastery in maths children need to be enabled to acquire a deep understanding of maths concepts, structures and procedures, step by step. Complex mathematical concepts are built on simpler conceptual components and when children understand every step in the learning sequence, maths becomes transparent and makes logical sense. Interactive lessons establish deep understanding in small steps, as well as effortless fluency in key facts such as counting and number bonds. The whole class works on the same content and no child is left behind.

Power Maths Reception

- Builds every concept in small, progressive steps.
- Combines a mastery approach with Early Years best practice.
- Provides the tools you need to develop growth mindsets.
- Establishes firm foundations for maths learning to enable children to succeed in KS1 and beyond.

The *Power Maths* approach

Everyone can!

Founded on the conviction that every child can achieve, *Power Maths* enables children to build number fluency, confidence and understanding, step by step.

Child-centred learning

Children master concepts one step at a time in lessons that embrace a Concrete-Pictorial-Abstract (C-P-A) approach, avoid overload, build on prior learning and help them see patterns and connections. Same-day intervention ensures sustained progress.

Continuing professional development

Embedded teacher support and development offer every teacher the opportunity to continually improve their subject knowledge and manage whole-class teaching for mastery.

Whole-class teaching

An interactive, whole-class teaching model encourages thinking and precise mathematical language and allows children to deepen their understanding as far as they can.

Your *Power Maths Reception* resources

Online subscription

The online subscription gives you access to a variety of helpful resources.

Online Flashcards

The **Online Flashcards** are the starting point for most *Power Maths Reception* lessons. They stimulate children's interest and introduce key mathematical concepts. The flashcards are designed for use on the interactive whiteboard to facilitate either whole class or small group sessions. These taught sessions take around 10–15 minutes per day, and include plenty of hands-on activities.

Teaching tools

From the **Online Flashcards**, you can launch interactive teaching tools that allow you to model and change the structures and representations used in *Power Maths*. This allows you to demonstrate the concept using a variety of examples, to ensure children gain a deep understanding.

Online versions of Teacher Guide pages

PDF pages give support at both unit and lesson levels.

Mathematical concept videos

Watch the professional development videos as you introduce each new concept to help you teach with confidence. The videos explore how the concept fits in and builds through Reception as well as common misconceptions and how to assess mastery.

Your *Power Maths Reception* resources

Maths Journals

The **Maths Journals** have been designed to support best practice in Early Years, whilst also providing evidence that each child has mastered a concept.

The journal activities can be guided or child-initiated, depending on your school's ethos.

Children are encouraged to choose how they demonstrate their understanding of the concept – those who are ready might write or draw their answers, but equally they may choose to place concrete objects on the page and move them around to demonstrate their understanding if they prefer. Any representation is fine, as long as it shows that they have understood the mathematical concept.

Children draw themselves on the front cover to personalise their **Maths Journal**.

Practice questions allow children to consolidate their understanding of the concept by drawing or using concrete objects.

Reflect questions allow children to demonstrate the depth of their understanding with a more open-ended question that provides opportunities for greater depth.

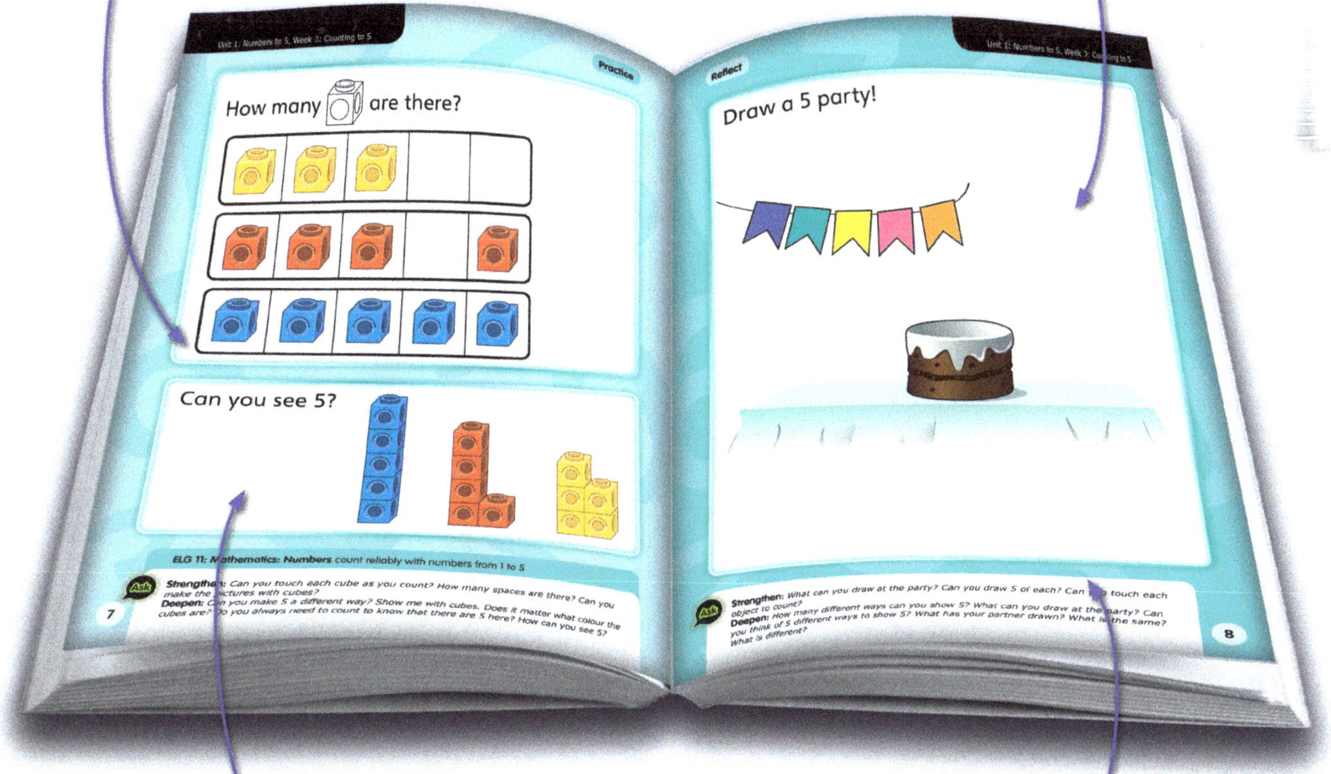

Activities are linked to Early Learning Goals.

Teacher Notes on the page give Teaching Assistants some useful prompt questions to support children who are yet to achieve mastery and to stretch children who are able to go deeper.

Your *Power Maths Reception* resources

Teacher Guides

Think of your **Teacher Guides** as *Power Maths* handbooks that will guide, support and inspire your day-to-day teaching. Clear and concise, and illustrated with helpful examples, your **Teacher Guides** will help you make the best possible use of every individual lesson. They also provide wrap-around professional development, enhancing your own subject knowledge and helping you to grow in confidence about moving your children forward together.

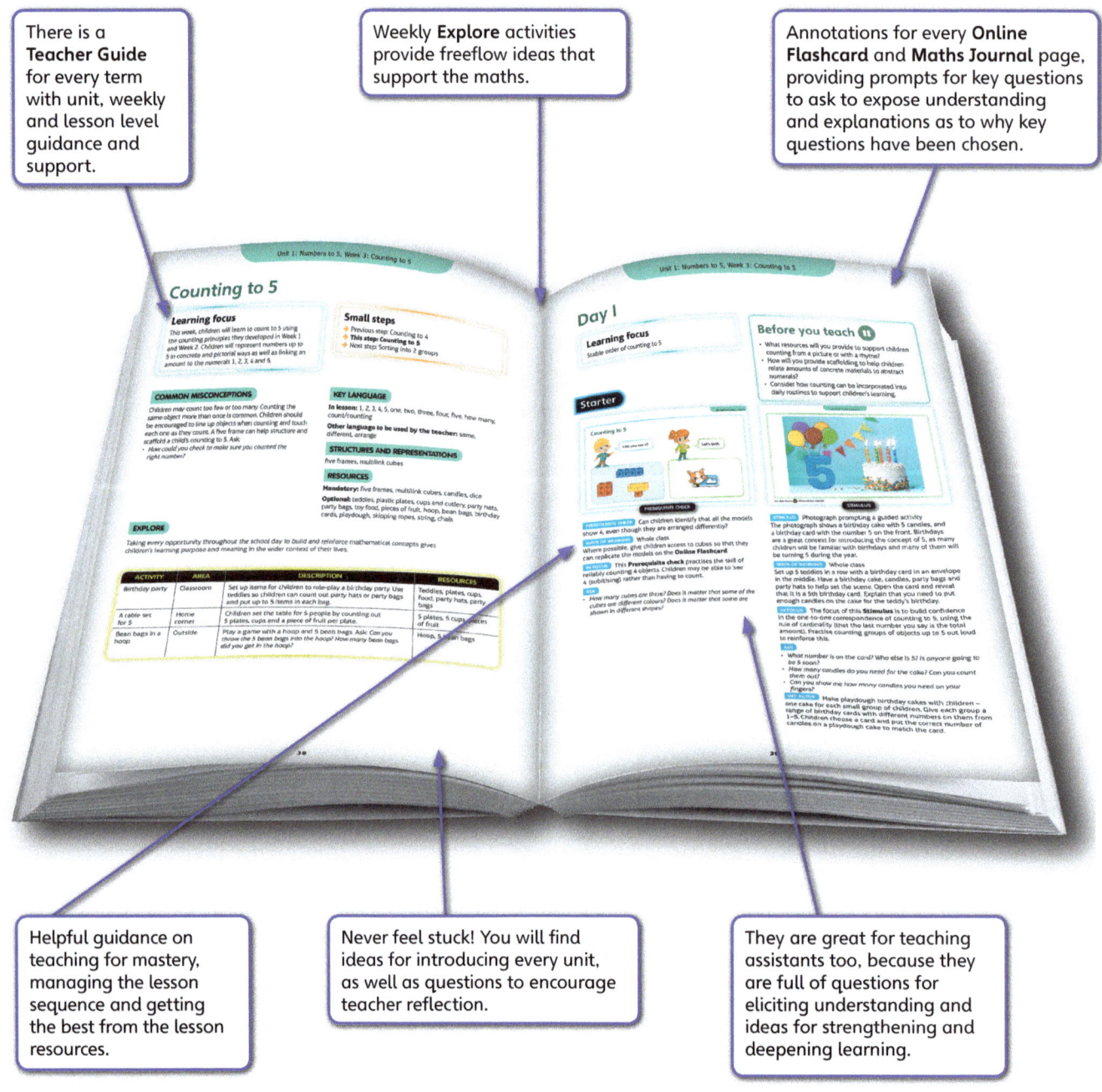

- There is a **Teacher Guide** for every term with unit, weekly and lesson level guidance and support.
- Weekly **Explore** activities provide freeflow ideas that support the maths.
- Annotations for every **Online Flashcard** and **Maths Journal** page, providing prompts for key questions to ask to expose understanding and explanations as to why key questions have been chosen.
- Helpful guidance on teaching for mastery, managing the lesson sequence and getting the best from the lesson resources.
- Never feel stuck! You will find ideas for introducing every unit, as well as questions to encourage teacher reflection.
- They are great for teaching assistants too, because they are full of questions for eliciting understanding and ideas for strengthening and deepening learning.

Power Maths Reception, yearly overview

Autumn term

Strand	Unit		Week	Weekly title	Early Learning Goal
Number – number and place value	Unit 1	Numbers to 5	1	Counting to 1, 2 and 3	Children count reliably with numbers from 1 to 20, place them in order.
			2	Counting to 4	
			3	Counting to 5	
Number – addition and subtraction	Unit 2	Sorting	4	Sorting into 2 groups	Children explore characteristics of everyday objects.
Number – number and place value	Unit 3	Comparing groups within 5	5	Comparing quantities of identical objects	Pre-requisite to: Using quantities and objects, they add and subtract 2 single-digit numbers and count on or back to find the answer.
			6	Comparing quantities of non-identical objects	
Number – addition and subtraction	Unit 4	Change within 5	7	One more	Say which number is one more or one less than a given number.
			8	One less	
Measurement	Unit 5	Time	9	My day	Children use everyday language to talk about time to solve problems.

Power Maths Reception, yearly overview

Spring term

Strand	Unit	Week	Weekly title	Early Learning Goal
Number – addition and subtraction	Unit 6	Number bonds within 5	1	Introducing the part-whole model	Pre-requisite to: Using quantities and objects, they add and subtract 2 single-digit numbers and count on or back to find the answer.
Number – number and place value	Unit 7	Numbers to 10	2	Counting to 6, 7 and 8	Children count reliably with numbers from 1 to 20, place them in order.
			3	Counting to 9 and 10	
Number – number and place value	Unit 8	Comparing numbers within 10	4	Comparing groups up to 10	Children explore characteristics of everyday objects.
Number – addition and subtraction	Unit 9	Addition to 10	5	Combining 2 groups to find the whole	Using quantities and objects, they add and subtract 2 single-digit numbers and count on or back to find the answer.
Number – addition and subtraction	Unit 10	Number bonds to 10	6	Using a ten frame	Pre-requisite to: Using quantities and objects, they add and subtract 2 single-digit numbers and count on or back to find the answer.
			7	The part-whole model to 10	
Geometry – properties of shape	Unit 11	Shape and space	8	Spacial awareness	Children explore characteristics of everyday objects and shapes and use mathematical language to describe them.
			9	3D shapes	
			10	2D shapes	

Power Maths Reception, yearly overview

Summer term

Strand	Unit		Week	Weekly title	Early Learning Goal
Geometry – properties of shape	Unit 12	Exploring patterns	1	Making simple patterns	Children recognise, create and describe patterns.
			2	Exploring more complex patterns	
Number – addition and subtraction	Unit 13	Counting on and counting back	3	Adding by counting on	Using quantities and objects, they add and subtract 2 single-digit numbers and count on or back to find the answer.
			4	Taking away by counting back	
Number – number and place value	Unit 14	Numbers to 20	5	Counting to 20	Children count reliably with numbers from 1 to 20, place them in order.
Number – multiplication and division	Unit 15	Numerical patterns	6	Doubling	They solve problems, including doubling, halving and sharing.
			7	Halving and sharing	
			8	Odds and evens	
Number – number and place value	Unit 16	Measure	9	Length, height and distance	Children use everyday language to talk about size, weight, capacity, position, distance, time and money to compare quantities and objects and to solve problems.
			10	Weight	
			11	Capacity	

Teaching sequence

Power Maths Reception is built around a weekly structure, with each new small step of learning introduced over the course of five lessons. There is enough flexibility in the termly plans to be able to spread out the five lessons over a longer period if you wish, however, we recommend that you work through the materials in the suggested order, as each new concept builds on what has been previously taught.

Each week is introduced in the **Teacher Guide** by an introduction page, which provides practical tips for the week's learning.

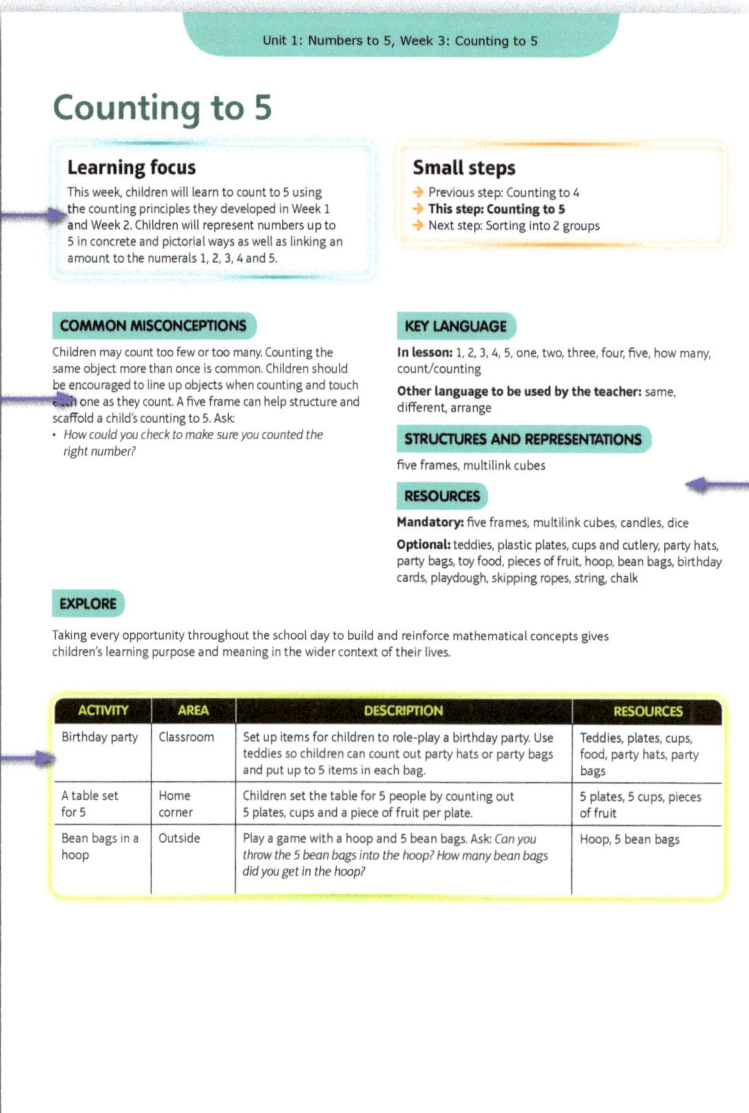

The **Learning focus** and **Small steps** help you to understand the key learning for the week and where it fits.

The **Common misconceptions** tells you the likely mistakes children may make and how you can counteract them to ensure children develop a firm understanding.

The **Explore** section provides a bank of ideas for activities you can set up in your classroom throughout the week, helping you to embed the maths concepts into everyday life.

The Introduction page explains the key language, structures and representations that will be introduced in the unit.

Day 1: Weekly starter

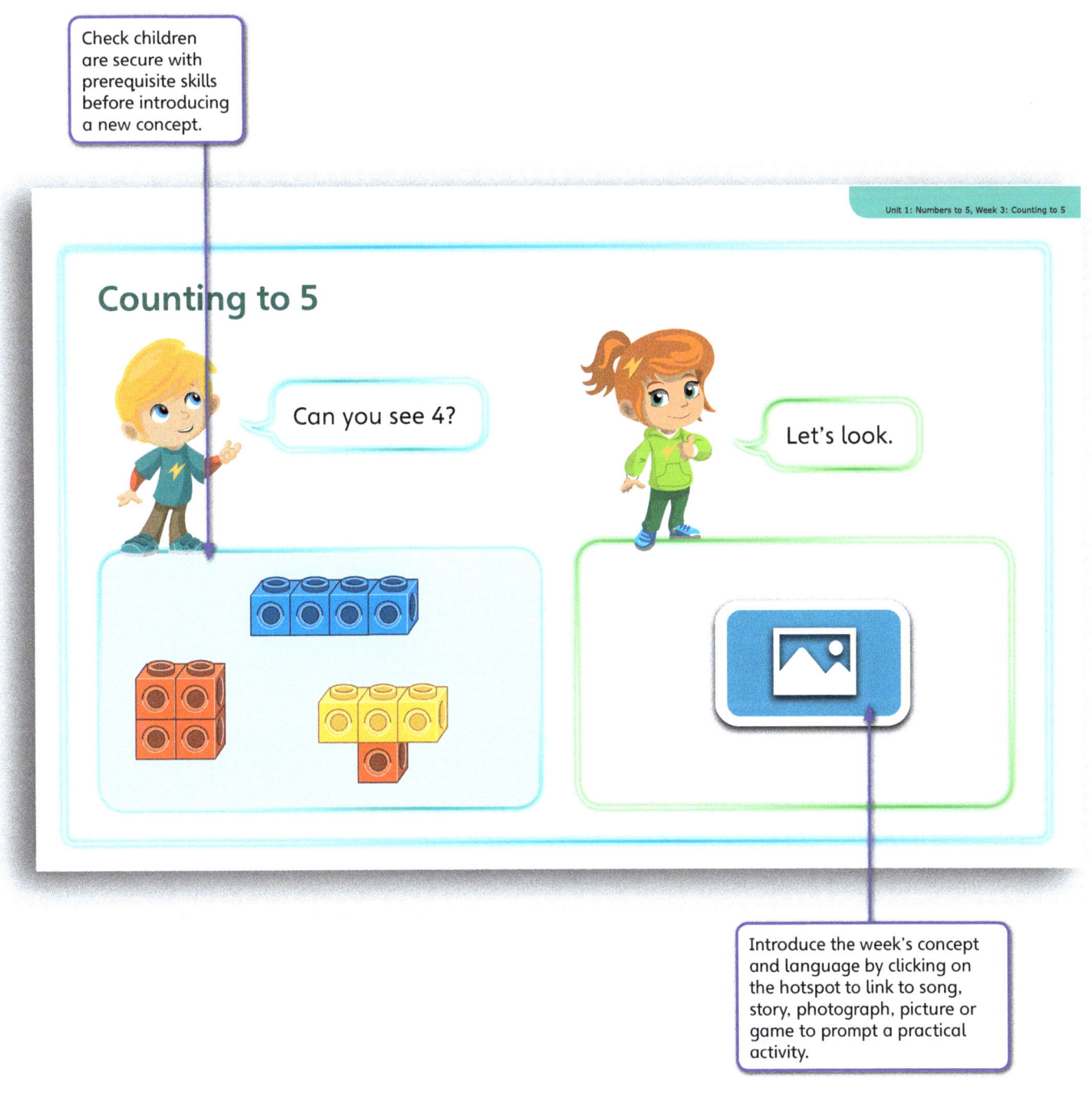

Day 2: Discover and Share

Children **Discover** the concept by attempting a practical problem set in a real-life context.

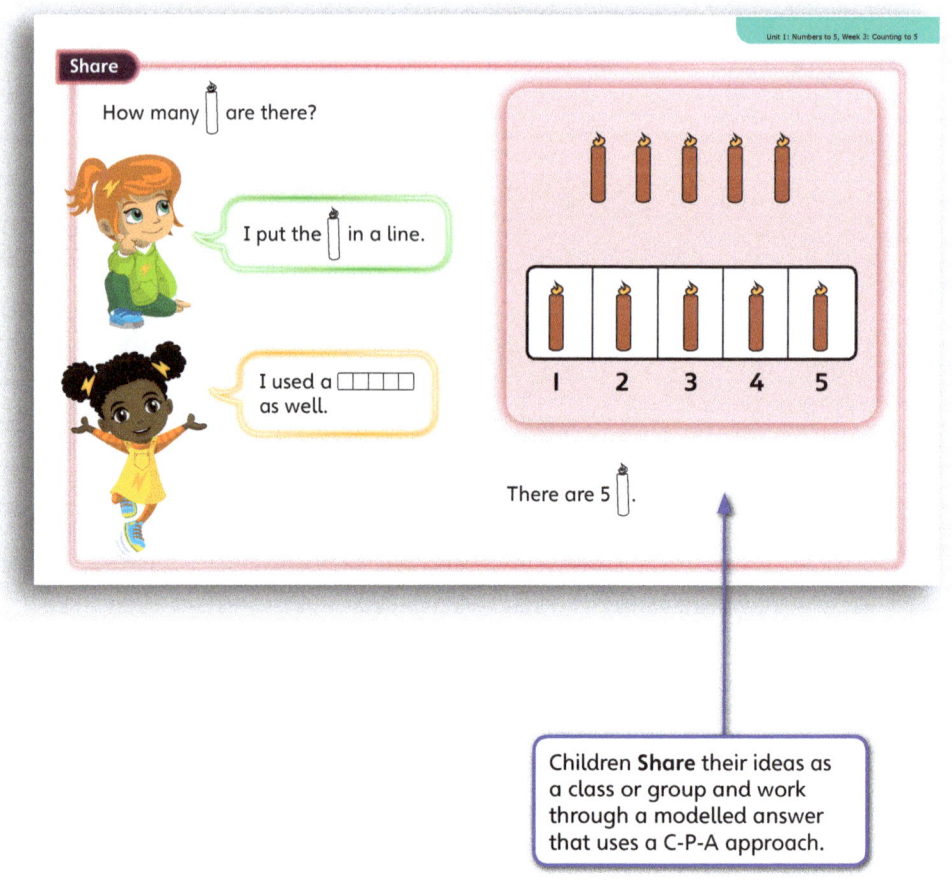

Children **Share** their ideas as a class or group and work through a modelled answer that uses a C-P-A approach.

Day 3: Think together and Practice

Think together provides whole-class guided practice opportunities and moves children on a step in their understanding.

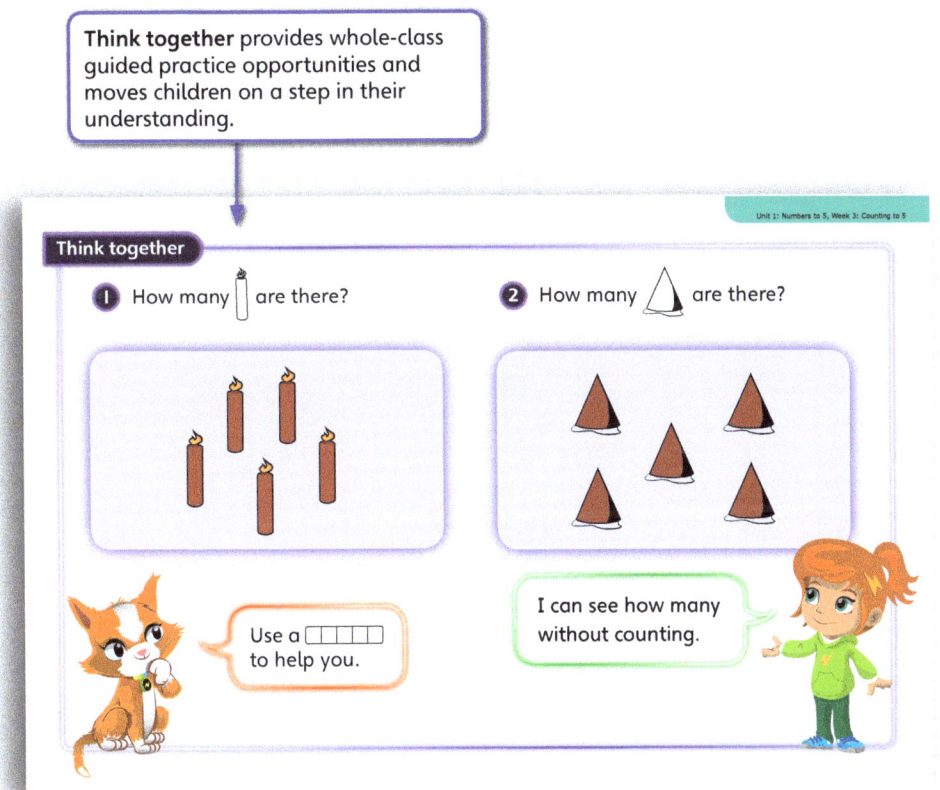

The **Maths Journal** provides an opportunity for independent practice. Children draw, use concrete objects or talk through the problem to show their understanding.

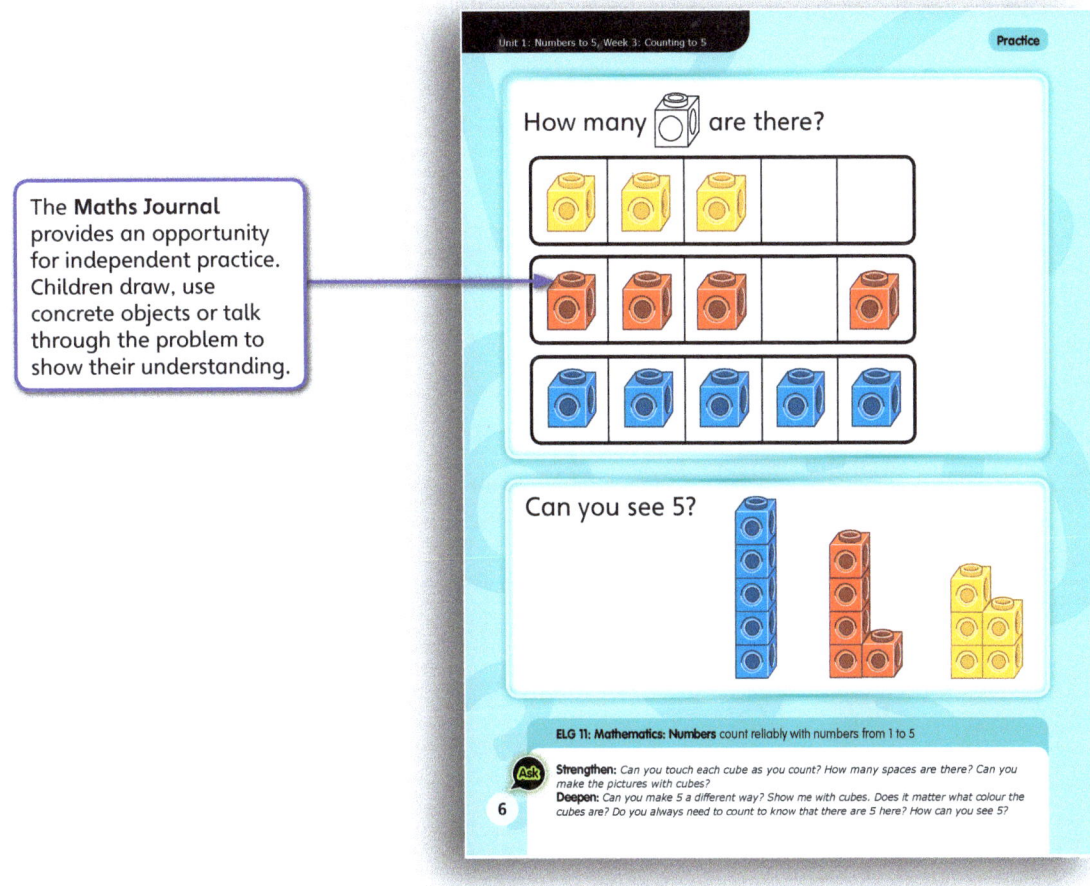

Day 4: Challenge and Strengthen

The whole class attempt the **Challenge**, which deepens children's understanding.

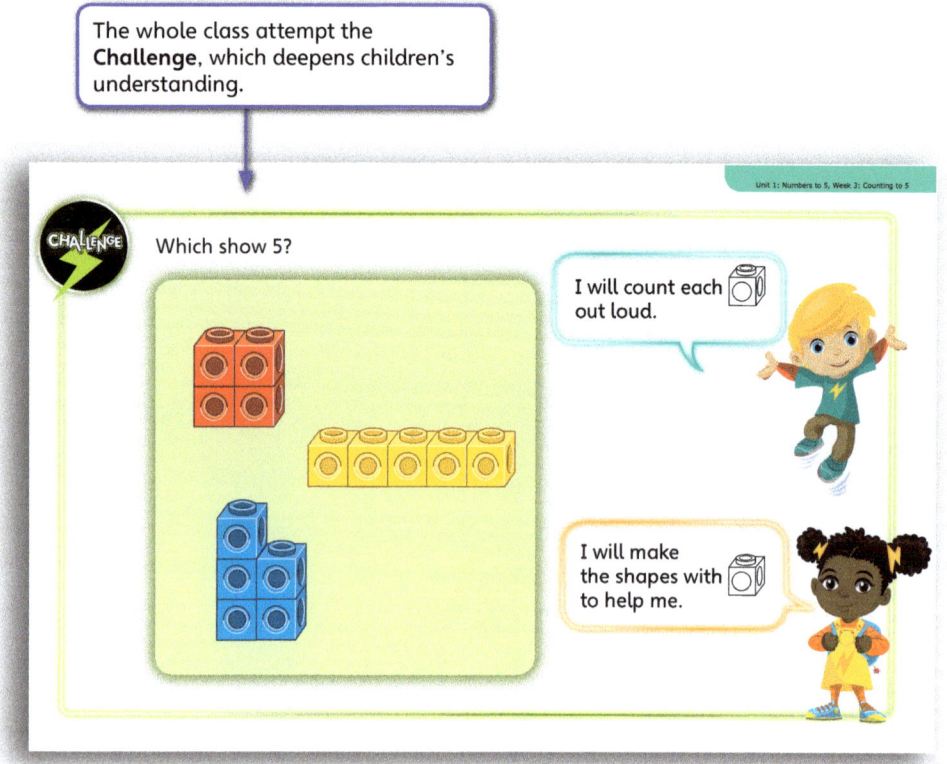

The **Teacher Guide** provides **Strengthen** activity ideas to support those who are not yet ready for the challenge, to help keep the class together.

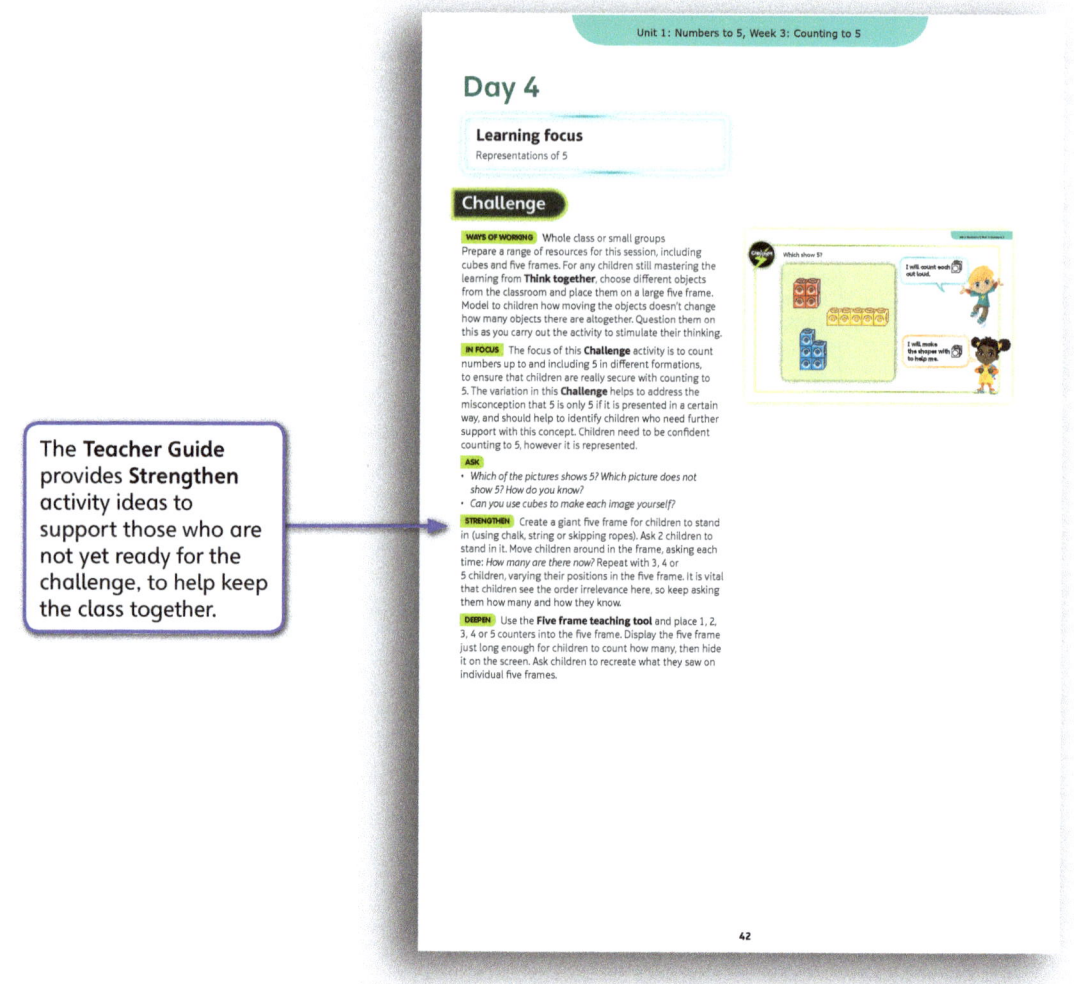

Day 5: Practical activities and Reflect

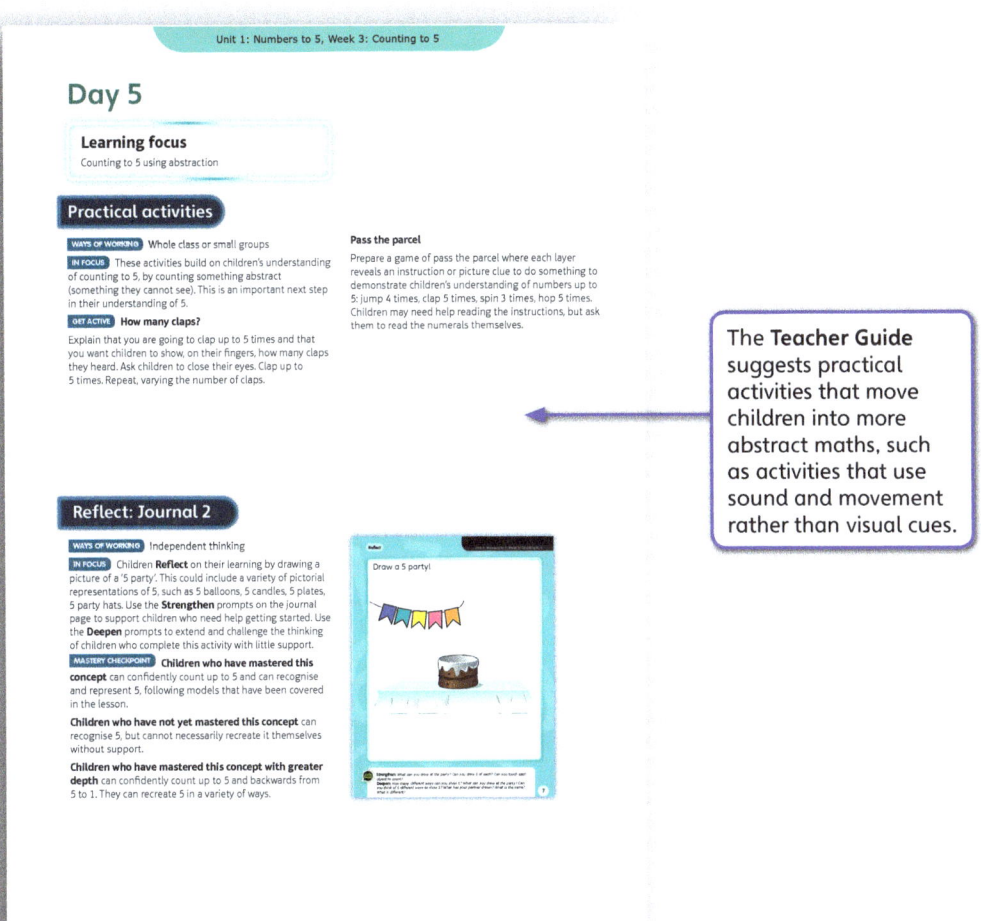

The **Teacher Guide** suggests practical activities that move children into more abstract maths, such as activities that use sound and movement rather than visual cues.

Children show the depth of their understanding in an open-ended **Reflect** activity in the **Maths Journal**. Children can show whether they have mastered the concept, and they also have the opportunity to demonstrate mastery with greater depth, for example by breaking the whole up in more than one way in the example shown.

Structures and representations

Unlike most other subjects, maths comprises a wide array of abstract concepts – and that is why children and adults so often find it difficult. By taking a Concrete-Pictorial-Abstract (C-P-A) approach, *Power Maths* allows children to tackle concepts in a tangible and more comfortable way.

Non-linear stages

Concrete

Replacing the traditional approach of a teacher working through a problem in front of the class, the concrete stage introduces real objects that children can use to 'do' the maths – any familiar object that a child can manipulate and move to help bring the maths to life. It is important to appreciate, however, that children must always understand the link between models and the objects they represent. For example, children need to first understand that three cakes could be represented by three pretend cakes, and then by three counters or bricks. Frequent practice helps consolidate this essential insight. Although they can be used at any time, good concrete models are an essential first step in understanding.

Pictorial

This stage uses pictorial representations of objects to let children 'see' what particular maths problems look like. It helps them make connections between the concrete and pictorial representations and the abstract maths concept. Children can also create or view a pictorial representation together, enabling discussion and comparisons. The *Power Maths* teaching tools are fantastic for this learning stage, and bar modelling is invaluable for problem solving throughout the primary curriculum.

Abstract

Our ultimate goal is for children to understand abstract mathematical concepts, signs and notation and, of course, some children will reach this stage far more quickly than others. To work with abstract concepts, a child needs to be comfortable with the meaning of, and relationships between, concrete, pictorial and abstract models and representations. The C-P-A approach is not linear, and children may need different types of models at different times. However, when a child demonstrates with concrete models and pictorial representations that they have grasped a concept, we can be confident that they are ready to explore or model it with abstract signs such as numbers and notation.

Use at any time and with any age to support understanding.

Applying the C-P-A approach in Reception

Concrete

Power Maths Reception introduces plenty of opportunities for concrete models in every lesson:

Discover always shows the maths set in a real-life, familiar context. Reception teachers are encouraged to use real, concrete versions of the objects to model the maths when introducing the **Discover** activity wherever possible, or toy versions of the objects. Children should be given the opportunity to handle and manipulate the objects during the **Discover** to help them to see, feel and manipulate the mathematical concepts.

The **Teacher Guide** suggests suitable concrete resources that children can use and manipulate, but you can add in other objects that you have available. Toys such as farm animals or dinosaurs, natural objects such as shells and leaves, and items found in the different classroom areas such as the home corner or sand tray are all great ways to introduce concrete objects into lessons.

If you don't have the suggested object to hand, get creative! Combine it with an art activity to get children to fashion the items out of playdough, such as playdough cakes, or copy and cut out pictures. Anything that gives children a clear link to the problem they are trying to solve, and allows them to physically pick up and move the objects around, will work.

Pictorial

Power Maths Reception introduces pictorial representations following a carefully thought-out progression. Initially, children begin by handling and counting multilink cubes, before learning to use these cubes to represent other things. The key representations introduced are:

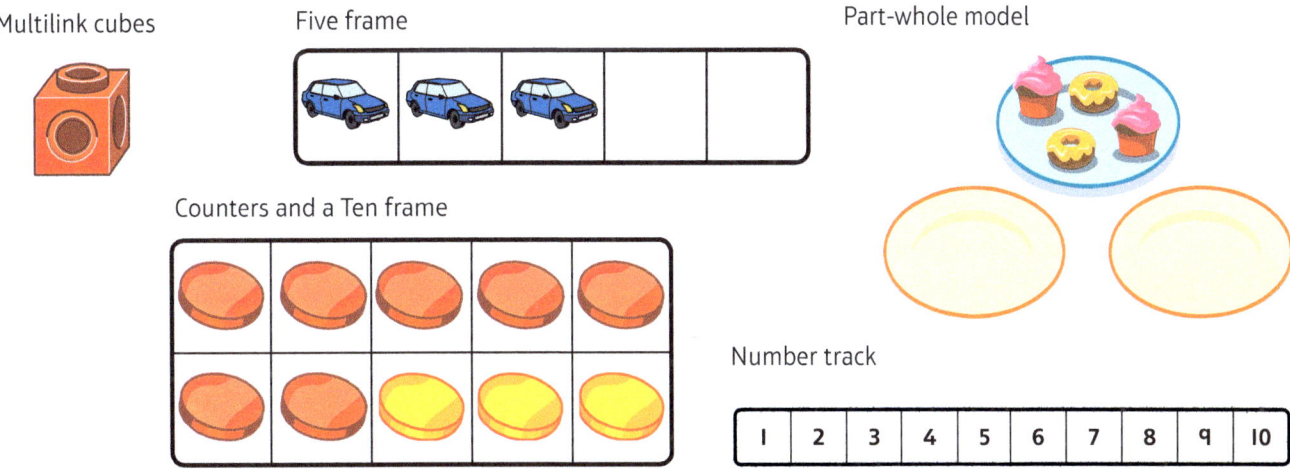

Abstract

Whilst our ultimate goal of children understanding abstract mathematical concepts, signs and notation may seem beyond the scope of Reception, children in the Early Years Foundation Stage can take steps towards building an abstract understanding. *Power Maths Reception* supports children to develop this understanding by:

- Presenting numerals alongside pictorial representations in the modelled answers in **Share** wherever relevant. Teachers should draw children's attention to these numerals during whole-class sessions, and ask children to practise associating the numerals with the numbers they represent.

- Providing large photocopiable numerals at the back of the **Teacher Guide** A (0–5) and **Teacher Guide** B (6–10), so that you can use these to support classroom displays for children to explore.

- Suggesting **Practical activities** towards the end of each week of teaching that begin to reduce children's reliance on visual representation. These activities include applying the maths concepts to sound and movement, meaning that children have to think in a more abstract way about the numbers – for example: *How many claps can you hear? One* …[pause] … *two, three*. Children are expected to count without relying on having counters or cubes to manipulate, moving them on a step towards more abstract thinking.

The *Power Maths* characters

The *Power Maths* characters model the traits of growth mindset learners and encourage resilience by prompting and questioning children as they work. Appearing frequently in the **Online Flashcards** and **Maths Journals**, they are your allies in teaching and discussion, helping to model methods, alternatives and misconceptions, and to prompt discussion. They encourage and support your children, too: they are all hardworking, enthusiastic and unafraid of making and talking about mistakes.

Meet the team!

Determined Dexter is resolute, resilient and systematic. He concentrates hard, always tries his best and he'll never give up – even though he doesn't always choose the most efficient methods!

Flexible Flo is open-minded and sometimes indecisive. She likes to think differently and come up with a variety of methods or ideas.

'Let's try again.'

'Mistakes are cool!'

'Have I found all of the solutions?'

'Let's try it this way …'

'Can we do it differently?'

'I've got another way of doing this!'

'I'm going to try this!'

'I know how to do that!'

'Want to share my ideas?'

Curious Ash is eager, interested and inquisitive, and he loves solving puzzles and problems. Ash asks lots of questions but sometimes gets distracted.

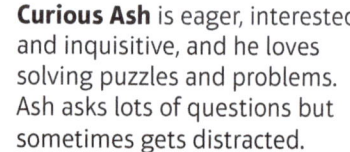

'What if we tried this …?'

'I wonder …'

'Is there a pattern here?'

Brave Astrid is confident, willing to take risks and unafraid of failure. She is never scared to jump straight into a problem or question, and although she often makes simple mistakes she is happy to talk them through with others.

Miaow!

Sparks the Cat

Mathematical language

Traditionally, we in the UK have tended to try simplifying mathematical language to make it easier for young children to understand. By contrast, evidence and experience show that by diluting the correct language, we actually mask concepts and meanings for children. We then wonder why they are confused by new and different terminology later down the line! *Power Maths* is not afraid of 'hard' words and avoids placing any barriers between children and their understanding of mathematical concepts. As a result, we need to be planned, precise and thorough in building every child's understanding of the language of maths. Throughout the **Teacher Guides** you will find support and guidance on how to introduce new mathematical language to young children.

Use the following key strategies to build children's mathematical vocabulary, understanding and confidence.

Precise and consistent

Everyone in the classroom should use the correct mathematical terms in full, every time. Used consistently, precise maths language will be a familiar and non-threatening part of children's everyday experience.

Full sentences

Teachers and children alike need to use full sentences to explain or respond. When children use complete sentences, it both reveals their understanding and embeds their knowledge.

Stem sentences

These important sentences help children express mathematical concepts accurately, and are used throughout the *Power Maths Reception* resources. Encourage children to repeat them frequently, whether working independently or with others. Examples of stem sentences are:

'4 is a part, 5 is a part, 9 is the whole.'

'There are … groups. There are … in each group.'

Key vocabulary

The unit starters highlight essential vocabulary for every lesson. New terminology is highlighted in bold on the **Online Flashcards** and the **Teacher Guide** lists important mathematical language for every unit and lesson, with new terms flagged in bold, and in the colour of the learning section in which they are introduced, once again.

Make maths part of everyday life

Use every opportunity to build mathematical vocabulary into everyday classroom life. For example, once Time has been introduced, ask children every day what they will do first, then and next today, and encourage them to use words such as *before* and *after*. the more normal you make mathematical language, the less intimidating it becomes.

Keeping the class together

Traditionally, children who learn quickly have been accelerated through the curriculum. As a consequence, their learning may be superficial and will lack the many benefits of enabling children to learn with and from each other.

By contrast, *Power Maths'* mastery approach values real understanding and richer, deeper learning above speed. It sees all children learning the same concept in small, cumulative steps, each finding and mastering challenge at their own level. Remember that when you teach for mastery, EVERYONE can do maths! Those who grasp a concept easily have time to explore and understand that concept at a deeper level. The whole class therefore moves through the curriculum at broadly the same pace via individual learning journeys.

For some teachers, the idea that a whole class can move forward together is revolutionary and challenging. However, the evidence of global good practice clearly shows that this approach drives engagement, confidence, motivation and success for all learners, and not just the high flyers. The strategies below will help you keep your class together on their maths journey.

Strengthen understanding

Use a wide variety of concrete materials to help children strengthen their understanding, and don't be afraid to take more time over a particular topic if you feel your class need it. For example, if *Power Maths Reception* has asked children to count 4 leaves, then set up activities where they need to count 4 pencils, pick out 4 toy cars from a bigger group, hand out 4 snacks, and so on ... anything to help them practise and consolidate their understanding. These activities can be built into everyday classroom life. The **Teacher Guide** provides some ideas for freeflow activities for each week to get you started, as well as **Strengthen** activities you can use as needed.

Deepen understanding

Power Maths Reception lessons offer many opportunities for you to deepen and broaden children's learning. The **Challenge** question each week gives all children an opportunity to explore concepts in greater depth. Children who have grasped concepts quickly should be encouraged to explore alternative solutions, for example, when partitioning a whole of 4 into 1 and 3, what other ways can they break the whole into parts? Could they split the whole into 3 parts? They should also be encouraged to reason and explain why something is true, and how they know they have found all the solutions. **Deepen** activities and questions appear throughout the **Teacher Guide** and in the **Ask** section in the **Maths Journals** to support you in deepening children's understanding.

Prepare to be surprised!

Children may grasp a concept quickly or more slowly. The 'fast graspers' won't always be the same individuals, nor does the speed at which a child understands a concept predict their success in maths. Are they struggling or just working more slowly?

Take cues from the characters

The *Power Maths* characters model mathematical thinking and ideas, and act as prompts for class discussion. They often make suggestions for strategies for tackling a problem as well as asking questions that prompt children to explore the concept in greater depth.

I can use to help me.

Variation helps visualisation

Children find it much easier to visualise and grasp concepts if they see them presented in a number of ways, so be prepared to offer and encourage many different representations.

For example, the number six could be represented in various ways:

Unit 1
Numbers to 5

Mastery Expert tip! "When teaching this unit, I used the contexts given in the pictures to make the maths as practical as possible. The children were far more confident about explaining their ideas when we were role-playing the concepts and making the maths relevant to their lives."

Don't forget to watch the Counting skills video!

ELGs

This unit supports the following ELGs:

→ **ELG 11: Mathematics: Numbers**
count reliably with numbers from 1 to 20, place them in order and say which number is one more or one less than a given number

→ **ELG 2: Communication and language: Understanding**
answer 'how' and 'why' questions about their experiences and in response to stories or events

WHY THIS UNIT IS IMPORTANT

This unit focuses on children's ability to recognise, represent and manipulate numbers to 5. Children begin by counting groups of objects up to 3, then 4, before looking at 5. Children will learn to recognise and count different representations of numbers up to 5 and use a five frame to help structure the counting and reasoning.

WAYS OF WORKING

Ensure there are five frames for children to use during this unit. Children can use five frames and real life objects alongside the **Online Flashcards** to help them understand the concepts.

WHERE THIS UNIT FITS

→ **Unit 1: Numbers to 5**
→ Unit 2: Sorting

In this unit, children will learn to count reliably to 5 and recognise the numerals 1, 2, 3, 4 and 5. They will begin to recognise different representations of numbers up to 5, such as those shown in a five frame and on dice, and to understand that even if the order or arrangement changes, the number stays the same.

Link to Key Stage 1

Number – number and place value

- count to and across 100, forwards and backwards, beginning with 0 or 1, or from any given number; count, read and write numbers to 100 in numerals; count in multiples of twos, fives and tens
- identify and represent numbers using objects and pictorial representations including the number line, and use the language of: equal to, more than, less than (fewer), most, least

The learning in this unit establishes methods of counting objects reliably and the concept that numbers can be shown in different representations, which sets a strong foundation for children working with larger numbers and quantities in KS1.

Unit 1: Numbers to 5

ASSESSING MASTERY

Children who have mastered this unit will be able to:
- count up to 5 objects reliably
- understand that numbers can be shown in different representations
- recognise the numerals 1, 2, 3, 4 and 5
- match groups of objects to the correct numeral

COMMON MISCONCEPTIONS	STRENGTHENING UNDERSTANDING	GOING DEEPER
Children may find counting backwards trickier and mistakenly count forwards instead.	Role-play situations where counting down is necessary, such as a rocket launch or blowing out birthday candles. Also sing songs like 'Five little monkeys' or 'Five little ducks'.	Count forwards round in a circle of up to five children. When the teacher shakes a tambourine switch to counting backwards.
Children may count too many or too few. They may count an object more than once or leave one out.	Encourage children to line up objects in a row and touch each object as they count.	Challenge children to count up to 5 objects from a larger group. Do they know when to stop counting?

STRUCTURES AND REPRESENTATIONS

Five frame: The five frames help to give children a sense of the numbers, and support their early understanding of number bonds to 5.

Multilink cubes: Multilink cubes provide a physical representation of an amount, which children can handle and move as they count to support their early counting skills.

RESOURCES

Mandatory: digit cards, five frame (photocopiable 7), multilink cubes, real life objects (buckets, spades, leaves, candles, party hats, plates or cups), dice, laminated print outs of numerals 1–5 (photocopiables 2–6)

Optional: any items that children can count (such as pencils, crayons, dice, natural objects) birthday cards, playdough, photos or drawings of groups to represent 1, 2 and 3, pictures of butterflies, camera, paper, pens, teddies, plastic plates, cups and cutlery, party hats, party bags, toy food, pieces of fruit, hoop, bean bags, role-play toys, skipping ropes, string, chalk

TEACHING TOOLS

five frame, multilink cubes

KEY LANGUAGE

There is some key language that children will need to know as part of the learning in this unit:
- 1, 2, 3, 4, 5, one, two, three, four, five, number
- count, count forwards, count backwards
- how many, total, altogether
- five frame, cube
- **same, different**
- next, after, arrange

Unit 1: Numbers to 5, Week 1: Counting to 1, 2 and 3

Counting to 1, 2 and 3

Learning focus

This week, children will start to count to 3 and back from 3. They will link the skill of counting 3 concrete objects to the pictorial representation of 3, and then to the abstract numerals 1, 2 and 3.

Small steps

→ **This step:** Counting to 1, 2 and 3
→ **Next step:** Counting to 4

COMMON MISCONCEPTIONS

Children may count too quickly, not focusing on the one-to-one correspondence. Reinforce the principle of counting each object and saying the corresponding name of the number out loud. Encourage children to move the object to the side as they count to help them make the physical link between object and number. Ask:
- *Can you move the object and count the number at the same time? How many are there? Count them all carefully.*

Children may be tempted to race ahead with their counting, without taking time to ensure they are saying each number in order. Check children have a stable counting order. Encourage children to say the full sequence of numbers out loud. Ask:
- *How many are there? Can you count them all?*

KEY LANGUAGE

In lesson: one, two, three, 1, 2, 3, different, same

Other language to be used by the teacher: count, forwards, backwards, how many, in total, altogether

RESOURCES

Mandatory: buckets and spades, laminated print outs of numerals 1–3 (photocopiables 2–4)

Optional: any resources for children to count, such as pencils, toy cars, building blocks, paper, pens, bean bags, apples etc, photos or drawings of groups to represent 1, 2 and 3, camera, paper, pens

EXPLORE

Taking every opportunity throughout the school day to build and reinforce mathematical concepts gives children's learning purpose and meaning in the wider context of their lives.

ACTIVITY	AREA	DESCRIPTION	RESOURCES
Matching groups of objects to a number	Classroom	Provide large numerals 1–3. Encourage children to collect groups of 1, 2 or 3 objects from around the classroom or the outside area. Ask them and place their collections with the correct numeral.	Groups of small objects for children to collect, large laminated numerals 1–3
1, 2, 3 display	Display board	Split a large display board into 3 sections. Number them with a large numeral, 1, 2 and 3, and a corresponding representation of this number. Ask children to bring or draw pictures that represent 1, 2 and 3 to stick them on to the relevant part of the board.	Large numerals 1–3, photos or drawings of groups to represent 1, 2 and 3, camera
Classroom rules	Classroom	Ask: *How many can play at the water table/sand pit/in the home area at one time?* Make signs with children to display in these areas using the numeral and a picture of the number of children, to indicate the number of children allowed to play in any of the areas at one time.	Paper, pens

Unit 1: Numbers to 5, Week 1: Counting to 1, 2 and 3

Day 1

Learning focus
Stable order of counting to 3

Before you teach
- How will you support children who do not know the number names 1, 2 and 3?
- How could you adapt the resources to support children who struggle to hold small objects?

Starter

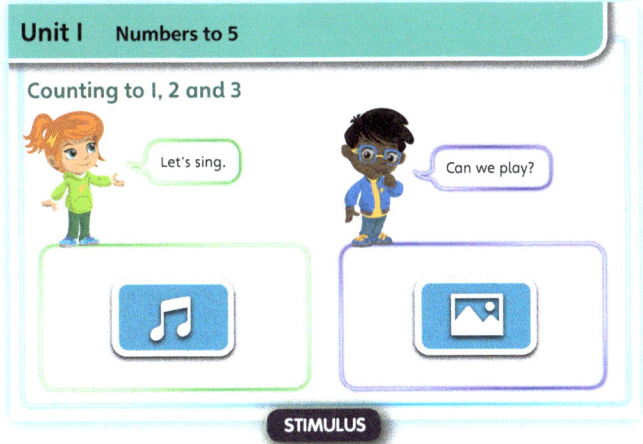

STIMULUS Song: 1, 2, 3

1, 2, 3

1, 2, 3, won't you sing along with me.
[Shout] 1, 2, 3!

1, 2, 3, won't you clap along with me.
[Shout] 1, 2, 3!

1, 2, 3, won't you hop along with me.
[Shout] 1, 2, 3!

WAYS OF WORKING Whole class
Introduce the concept of counting to 3 by listening to and singing the song with the whole class, encouraging them to join in with the actions.

IN FOCUS The song in this **Starter** is a good opportunity to stimulate the stable order of counting to 3. The numbers 1, 2 and 3 are introduced to children who have not come across them before.

ASK
- *What numbers did you hear? '1, 3, 2' – is that the right order? How do you say them in the right order? Tell me how to count*

to 3.

STIMULUS Photograph prompting a game
The photograph launched from the hotspot shows children doing an action in response to the teacher. Use this as a stimulus for introducing a simple 'countdown from 3' game.

WAYS OF WORKING Whole class
Stand at the front of the class and give children a simple instruction such as: *Touch your nose – 3, 2, 1*. Next, individual children take it in turns to stand at the front of the class and give an instruction, followed by the countdown: *3, 2, 1*. Children should complete the action straight after saying 1. This is similar to the familiar 'ready, steady, go'.

IN FOCUS The game offers a good opportunity to embed the stable order of counting to and back from 3. The game builds on understanding of the concept that numbers can go forwards and backwards.

ASK
- *What is the same and what is different with the counting this time? When should you do the action?*

GET ACTIVE In a large indoor or outdoor space, encourage children to continue the game in the **Starter** by doing an action (hop, jump, touch the ground, arm stretches) 3 times, counting up as they go. Say: *Do 3 hops, 3, 2, 1 go: hop, hop, hop* as they shout *1, 2, 3* – one hop per count.

Unit 1: Numbers to 5, Week 1: Counting to 1, 2 and 3

Day 2

Learning focus
One-to-one correspondence to 3

Discover

WAYS OF WORKING Whole class or small groups
Use every opportunity throughout the school day to count to and back from 3 with children. Ensure spades are available for children to use today.

IN FOCUS This **Discover** picture provides an opportunity to reinforce the stable order of counting. Some children may already be able to count to 3, but truly mastering the skill of one-to-one correspondence will help children when they start to work with higher numbers later on in the term. The question *How many spades are there?* introduces the concept of cardinality: how the last number in the count represents the total amount.

ASK
- What else can you see in the picture?
- How many buckets are there? How many children are there? How many flags are there in the sandcastle?

STRENGTHEN Ensure children use actual objects to represent the pictures. Teachers could set up the scenario presented in the **Discover** picture in the sand area so children can act out the problem.

DEEPEN Use guided prompt questions to more deeply embed children's understanding of one-to-one correspondence. Ask: *Can every child have a bucket? Can every child have a spade? How do you know?*

Share

WAYS OF WORKING Whole class

IN FOCUS **Share** introduces lining up objects to count them and presents the abstract numerals 1, 2 and 3 for the first time.

ASK
- How might you count these?
- Refer to what Flo is saying: *Can you use spades to help you? Why does it help to line them up?*
- Refer to what Dexter is saying: *Why does touching each spade make it easier to count? How do you know how many there are altogether?*
- Point to the numbers: *Do you recognise these? What do you call them? Have you seen them anywhere before? What do they mean? How do they link to the picture?*

STRENGTHEN Refer children to what Flo is saying. Encourage them to use three real spades. Next, look at what Dexter is saying and prompt children to touch each spade as they count, to ensure they link what they're saying with the physical representation of the number.

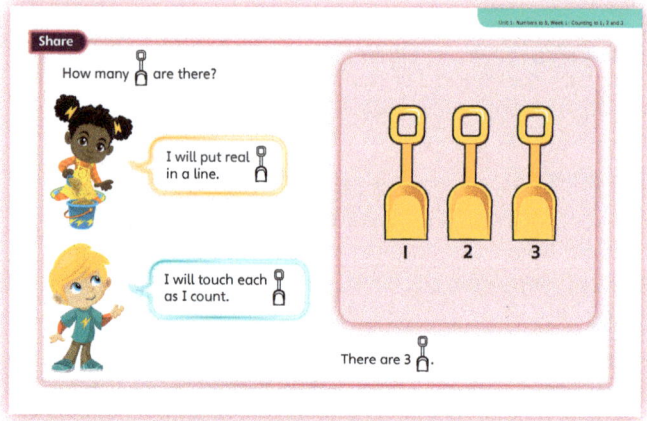

DEEPEN Encourage reasoning skills. Ask: *Are you counting forwards or backwards? How do you know? If the spades are in a different order, how many are there now? How do you know?* Look for children who immediately respond that there is the same total, even if they are in a different order.

GET ACTIVE Go to the sand area. Ask: *How many buckets are in the sand area? How many spades? What other objects are in the sand area? Can you count the different objects?*

28

Unit 1: Numbers to 5, Week 1: Counting to 1, 2 and 3

Day 3

Learning focus
Cardinality to 3

Think together

WAYS OF WORKING Whole class or small groups

To help prepare for the **Think together**, ask children to sit in a circle. Put two buckets in the middle of the circle, both the right way up. Ideally the buckets should be identical except for their colour. Discuss what is the same and what is different about the way the buckets look. Are they the same size? Are they the same colour? How many are there? Swap their positions over, so that children count the one that was previously number 2 first. What has changed? How many are there now? Move the buckets again, so there is a bigger gap between them. What has changed? How many are there now?

IN FOCUS Questions ❶ and ❷ help to reinforce the concept of the cardinality of numbers: understanding that arranging the same objects in different ways does not affect the number of objects.

ASK
- Question ❶: *What does 'how many' mean? What do you need to do to find the answer?*
- Question ❶: *If you count 1 and 1, how many are there altogether? What could you use to help you? Are the real buckets the same as the ones in the picture? Does it matter?*
- Question ❷: *How many buckets are there in this picture? How do you know? Could you move the buckets apart? Would there still be two?*

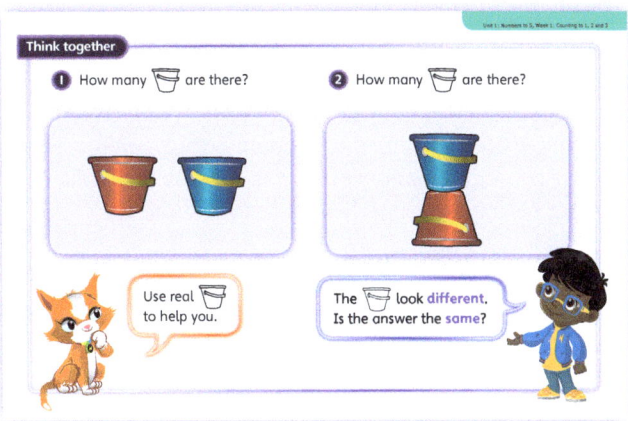

STRENGTHEN Use real buckets to recreate the pictures. Encourage children to touch the buckets as they count and develop a rhythm of counting finishing with a full sentence, for example: *1* [touch bucket], *2* [touch bucket]. *There are 2 buckets*. Start with buckets that are the same size and colour before using buckets that are different colours and sizes.

DEEPEN Put more than 3 buckets or other objects in the sand tray and ask children to count out 1, 2 or 3 from a larger group. The objects might be different colours or sizes so children can choose similar objects to count out, for example: *1, 2. There are 2 red spades. 1, 2, 3. There are 3 spades altogether.*

Practice: Journal 1

WAYS OF WORKING Independent thinking

IN FOCUS In this **Practice** activity, children can use real objects to help them count. The objects are now different sizes or in a different position to deepen children's thinking. Encourage them to count the objects and then say how many objects there are altogether in a full sentence, for example: *1, 2, 3. There are 3 buckets.*

MASTERY CHECKPOINT Can children answer both parts? If children are struggling with the first part, they may need more support with one-to-one correspondence. If they find the second part challenging, give them more opportunities to practise counting everyday objects. Encourage children to touch or move objects as they count them, and say the number out loud.

29

Day 4

Learning focus

Representations to 3

Challenge

WAYS OF WORKING Whole class or small groups

Only move children on to the **Challenge** if they have mastered the one-to-one correspondence of objects to numbers. If they need further support in this, continue to practise counting a variety of objects, and reinforce this learning before exposing them to the variation.

IN FOCUS This **Challenge** focuses on examples and non-examples of 3, and the fact that 3 can look different but still be 3. Use this activity to check that children are able to identify 3 when shown a variety of representations and orientations.

ASK

- *Have you found all the 3s in the picture? Are you sure?* [Guide children towards the wheels on the tricycle if they haven't counted those yet.]
- *Which picture doesn't show 3?*
- *What's the same and what's different about the pictures? Which picture is the odd one out?* [This could be any of them, but children should offer justifications for their choices.]

STRENGTHEN In small groups, make 3 using cubes. Move the cubes further apart. Ask: *Is it still 3? How do you know?* Put the cubes in different positions and use different colours and sizes of cubes to strengthen understanding.

DEEPEN Encourage children to become number detectives. Ask them to walk around the classroom and find objects in groups of 2 or 3. Refer to the **Explore** section on page 26 for activity ideas.

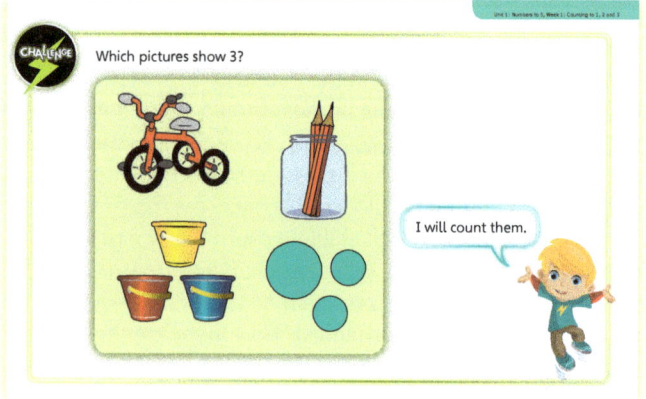

Day 5

Learning focus

Counting to 3 using abstraction

Practical activities

WAYS OF WORKING Whole class or small groups

IN FOCUS These activities introduce the numbers 1, 2 and 3 as an abstract concept. Encourage children to think about how they know a number is 1, 2 or 3 if they cannot see it or touch it.

GET ACTIVE 1, 2, 3

Link back to the song in the **Starter**. Talk to children about the second verse. Ask: *If I clap, can you tell me how many claps there are?* Experiment with a different number of claps (up to 3). Vary the pause between the claps. Clap, pause for a few seconds and then clap twice. Ask: *How many claps now?* Next, ask children to close their eyes and say out loud the number of claps you make. Encourage some of the children to take turns being the ones to clap while the rest of the class close their eyes and say the number of claps out loud.

How many did I drop?

Find an empty tin or other metal container and slowly drop some coins into it (up to 3). Ask: *How many did I drop? How do you know?* Add variation by changing the number of coins you drop, and by varying the pause between the drops.

Reflect: Journal 2

WAYS OF WORKING Independent thinking

IN FOCUS The focus of this **Reflect** activity is to review learning that has taken place this week. Can children confidently demonstrate their understanding of 3? Encourage them to place 3 physical objects on the page.

STRENGTHEN Use **Strengthen** ideas from the **Challenge** activity, and activities from **Explore**, to help embed ideas for children who have not yet mastered this concept. Keep practising 1, 2, 3 throughout the week to reinforce the language in a range of familiar contexts. Look out for children who still need to touch each object and have not started to subitise the number 3.

MASTERY CHECKPOINT **Children who have mastered this concept** can recognise and represent 3, following models that have been covered in the lesson.

Children who have not yet mastered this concept can recognise 3, but cannot necessarily recreate it. Look at a range of photographs: can they pick 1, 2 or 3 things from them?

Children who have mastered this concept with greater depth can recreate 3 in a variety of ways.

31

Unit 1: Numbers to 5, Week 2: Counting to 4

Counting to 4

Learning focus
This week, children will build on their knowledge of counting to 3, by counting to 4. They will link the skill of counting 4 concrete objects to the pictorial representation of 4, and then to the abstract numeral 4. The five frame is introduced for the first time.

Small steps
→ Previous step: Counting to 1, 2 and 3
→ **This step: Counting to 4**
→ Next step: Counting to 5

COMMON MISCONCEPTIONS
Children may still count too quickly, and not focus on the one-to-one correspondence of counting each object, resulting in either missing numbers in the sequence, miscounting or not recognising that the last number said is the number of objects. Ask:
- *How many are there? Can you count them all? What number are you going to start counting from?*
- *What was the last number you said? What number comes after …?*
- *Can you move the object or pick it up when you count it?*

KEY LANGUAGE
In lesson: one, two, three, four, 1, 2, 3, 4, cubes, how many, five frame

Other language to be used by the teacher: count, forwards, next, after, total, altogether, number

STRUCTURES AND REPRESENTATIONS
multilink cubes, five frames

RESOURCES
Mandatory: multilink cubes, objects to count, five frames

Optional: digit cards, groups of countable objects, including natural objects, paper, pens, large printed numbers 1–4 (photocopiables 2–5), role-play toys, pictures of butterflies

EXPLORE
Taking every opportunity throughout the school day to build and reinforce mathematical concepts gives children's learning purpose and meaning in the wider context of their lives.

ACTIVITY	AREA	DESCRIPTION	RESOURCES
Match the number	Classroom	Provide large laminated numerals 1–4. Encourage children to collect groups of 1, 2, 3 or 4 objects from around the classroom or the outside area. Ask them to place their collections with the correct number card.	Large printed numbers 1–4, variety of objects to collect
Collect 4	Outside	Children collect 4 natural objects, such as fallen leaves or conkers.	Items from nature
Groups of 4	Classroom	Encourage children to play and work in groups of 4. Ask: *How many children need to be in your group? How many children are in your group?*	Paper, pens
Set the table	Home corner	Ask children to set the table for 4 children. Ask: *How many plates will you need? How many forks? Can you get 4 cups?*	Role-play toys

Unit 1: Numbers to 5, Week 2: Counting to 4

Day 1

Learning focus
Stable order of counting to 4

Before you teach
- Can children count to 3?
- Can children count up to 3 objects reliably?
- Are children confident with resources and representations used in Week 1?

Starter

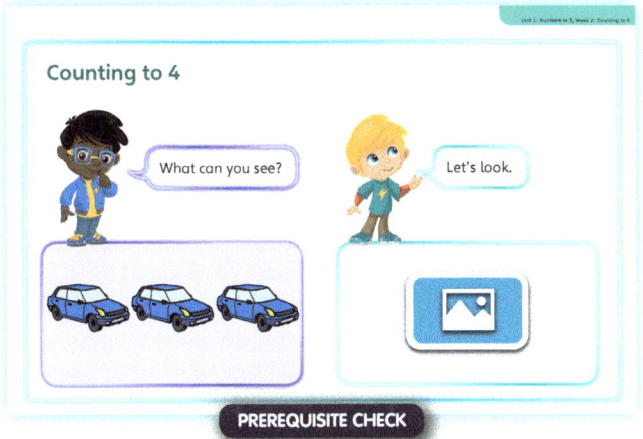

PREREQUISITE CHECK

PREREQUISITE CHECK Check that children can reliably count the 3 cars.

WAYS OF WORKING Whole class
Provide children with toy cars to count if needed.

IN FOCUS This **Prerequisite check** revisits stable order of counting to 3.

ASK
- *How many cars are there?*
- *How can you count them?*

STIMULUS

STIMULUS Photograph prompting a guided activity
The photograph shows 4 autumnal leaves on the grass. Encourage discussion about where children might see this in real life in the hope that this will lead to them looking for and counting autumnal objects in the outdoor provision or at playtimes.

WAYS OF WORKING Whole class

IN FOCUS This activity offers a good opportunity to stimulate the stable order of counting to 4.

ASK
- *What does 'how many' mean?*
- *Where are the leaves? Can you point to them?*
- *How are you going to count the leaves?*
- *What number do you start counting at?*
- *What number comes after …?*

GET ACTIVE Go outside and find leaves to match the image. Ask: *What other autumnal items can you find? Can you count them?*

Unit 1: Numbers to 5, Week 2: Counting to 4

Day 2

Learning focus
One-to-one correspondence to 4

Discover

WAYS OF WORKING Whole class or small groups

IN FOCUS Reinforce the stable order of counting by continuing to practise the skill of one-to-one correspondence, which will help children when they start working with higher numbers.

Discover also focuses on the cardinality of 4: that 4 is the last number you say in the count, so shows how many there are. Children are encouraged to be able to see 4 without having to count (subitising), by looking at different representations of 4.

ASK
- *How can you count the leaves?*
- *What else can you see in the picture?*
- *How many ladybirds are there? How many spots does the ladybird have? How did you count them? Did you need to count each spot? Can you count by looking, without counting each one?*
- *How many butterflies are there? How do you know? Does it matter that they are different sizes?*

DEEPEN Encourage children to find different things around the classroom that represent 4 and compare them with a partner's collection.

Share

WAYS OF WORKING Whole class

IN FOCUS The abstract numerals to 3 are revisited, continuing with the abstract numeral 4. Children are introduced to the five frame to represent amounts for the first time.

ASK
- *What number do you start counting on? What number do you finish counting on? So, how many leaves are there?*
- *Can you see how many leaves there are without counting each one?*
- *How does the five frame help you to count the number of leaves?*

STRENGTHEN Use actual leaves to support counting. Encourage children to touch each leaf as they count to reinforce one-to-one correspondence of numbers.

DEEPEN Encourage reasoning skills in this session by asking children: *Are you counting forwards or backwards? How do you know? When you count the number of leaves out loud, is the last number you say the total number? Show me. How do you know?*

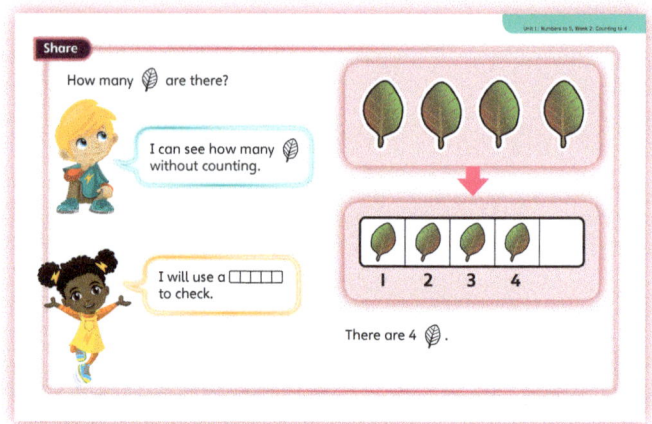

GET ACTIVE Go outside and ask children to collect groups of 2, 3 or 4 objects, such as fallen leaves or conkers. Count together, count in pairs, count forwards, count backwards. Match the amount in each group to a digit card. Mix the digit cards up and ask children to put them back in the right places.

Unit 1: Numbers to 5, Week 2: Counting to 4

Day 3

Learning focus
Cardinality to 4

Think together

WAYS OF WORKING Whole class or small groups
Give children a five frame and pictures of butterflies for Question ❶ and cubes for Question ❷.

IN FOCUS Cardinality of numbers: understanding that the last number used to count a group of objects represents how many are in the group.

ASK
- Question ❶: *Can you remember what 'how many' means? What do you need to do to find the answer? Does it matter that the butterflies are different sizes? Why not? Can you show the butterflies on a five frame?*
- Question ❷: *How many cubes are there? How do you know? Does it matter that they are one on top of the other? Show this with your cubes. Can you show the cubes on a five frame?*

STRENGTHEN Focus on saying the numbers out loud as you count to reinforce that the last number children say in a count is the total amount. Give as many opportunities to use the five frame as possible, choosing different real life objects to put on the five frame to count.

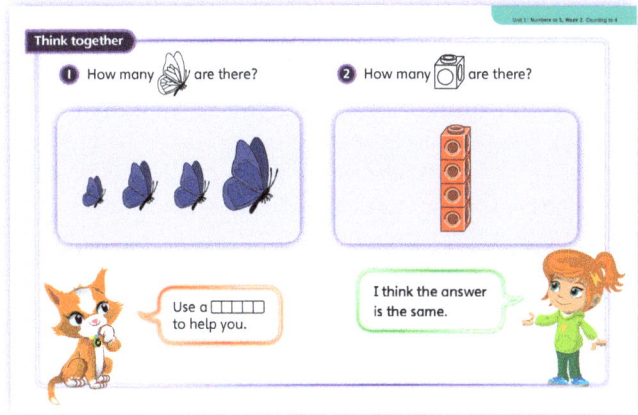

DEEPEN Extend children's thinking by using similar objects with slight variation, for example: 3 red cubes and 1 yellow cube. Ask: *How many cubes are there? Does it matter what colour the cubes are? What if 2 are red and 2 are blue, are there still 4? What if you line them up like this* (vertically), *or this* (in a 2 × 2 array)? *How do you know that the total amount stays the same?* [None have been added or removed.]

Practice: Journal I

WAYS OF WORKING Independent thinking

IN FOCUS In the first part of the **Practice** activity, children use pictures of butterflies to count how many altogether. In the second part, children look at different ways to represent numbers on a five frame.

MASTERY CHECKPOINT Can children count to 4 accurately? Can children use the five frame to represent the objects? Do children recognise that the final number in the count is the total? Can children record the total correctly?

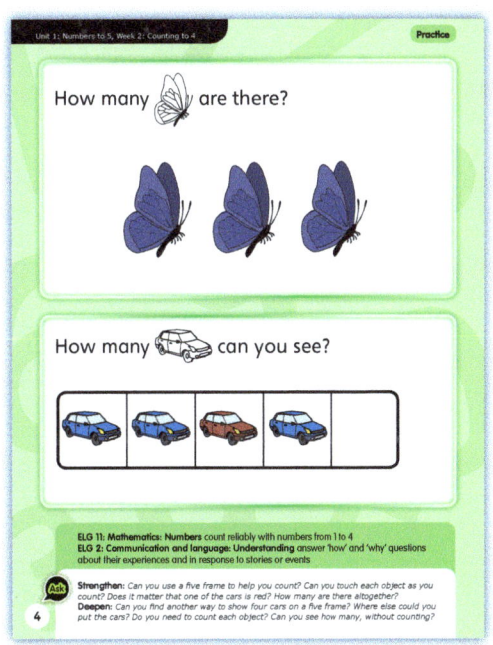

35

Unit 1: Numbers to 5, Week 2: Counting to 4

Day 4

Learning focus

Representations of 4

Challenge

WAYS OF WORKING Whole class or pairs
Guide children who need more support.

IN FOCUS The focus of this **Challenge** is for children to identify 4 from examples and non-examples of 4 and to familiarise them with the concept that 4 can look different but still be 4. This activity enables children to identify 4 using a variety of representations and orientations, and prompts them to 'see' 4 (subitising), rather than always having to count 4 things.

ASK

- *Have you found all the 4s in the picture? Are you sure?* [Guide children towards the points on the leaf if they have not counted those yet.]
- *Does it matter what colour the cubes are? If each cube is a different colour, is this still 4? What about if you move them into different places – is this still 4? How do you know?*
- *Can you see 4 in any of these pictures, without having to count each object? Show me where.*

DEEPEN Encourage children to be number 4 detectives. Go around the classroom in groups of 4 and identify objects that are in 4s. Children take photos of, or put labels on, the objects they find.

Embed understanding of order irrelevance: that 4 of something is still 4, whichever order it is presented in. Use the **Five frame teaching tool** to present objects in different variations, for example, different colours or occupying different positions. Ask: *Is this still 4?* [Change the colour of one object.] *Is this still 4?* [Move an object to a different position on the five frame.] *How many now?*

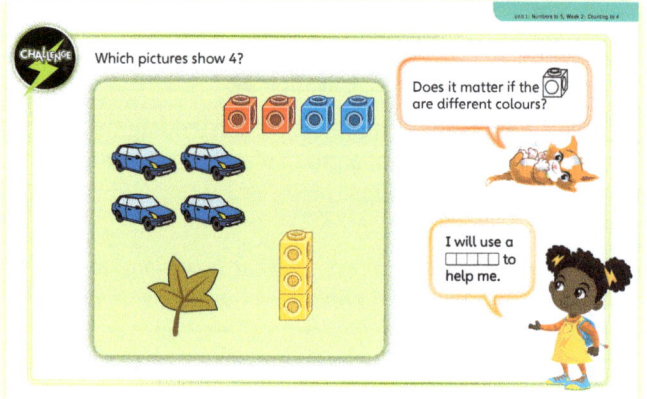

Unit 1: Numbers to 5, Week 2: Counting to 4

Day 5

Learning focus
Counting to 4 using abstraction

Practical activities

WAYS OF WORKING Whole class

IN FOCUS **Practical activities** can introduce the number 4 as an abstract concept. It is important that children make the link from the concrete and pictorial representations of an amount to the numeral '4' that represents the amount, and then the ways in which this amount can be represented in abstract form, for example, by making 4 claps.

GET ACTIVE **Listen to me clap**

Listen to me clap [clap 4 times]. *How many claps did I do? Can you clap 4 times?* Vary the speed of claps and the pauses between. Ask: *Is this still 4?* Ask children to perform other physical activities such as hopping, marching, spinning, jumping and waving. Each action should be performed up to 4 times and with varying speeds and pauses between.

Reflect: Journal 2

WAYS OF WORKING Independent thinking

IN FOCUS This activity gives children the opportunity to investigate the different ways they can make 4 on a five frame. Prompt children to represent the problem using cubes on a blank five frame. Next, encourage them to use a systematic approach to show all the ways to show 4 on a five frame. Ask: *Can you move just one cube to a different space? Now move a different cube.*

MASTERY CHECKPOINT **Children who have mastered this concept** can count reliably up to 4 objects and show 4 in a variety of ways using representations and resources used throughout the week.

Children who have not yet mastered this concept need support and scaffolding to show 4 and rely on resources and representations used throughout the week.

Children who have mastered this concept with greater depth can count up to 4 and show 4 in a variety of ways using a range of the resources and pictures used throughout the week and examples of their own. Children can talk about 4 in the wider world, for example, objects in the classroom, things at home, their age, the number of pets they have and so on.

37

Unit 1: Numbers to 5, Week 3: Counting to 5

Counting to 5

Learning focus

This week, children will learn to count to 5 using the counting principles they developed in Week 1 and Week 2. Children will represent numbers up to 5 in concrete and pictorial ways as well as linking an amount to the numerals 1, 2, 3, 4 and 5.

Small steps

- Previous step: Counting to 4
- **This step: Counting to 5**
- Next step: Sorting into 2 groups

COMMON MISCONCEPTIONS

Children may count too few or too many. Counting the same object more than once is common. Children should be encouraged to line up objects when counting and touch each one as they count. A five frame can help structure and scaffold a child's counting to 5. Ask:
- *How could you check to make sure you counted the right number?*

KEY LANGUAGE

In lesson: 1, 2, 3, 4, 5, one, two, three, four, five, how many, count/counting

Other language to be used by the teacher: same, different, arrange

STRUCTURES AND REPRESENTATIONS

five frames, multilink cubes

RESOURCES

Mandatory: five frames, multilink cubes, candles, dice

Optional: teddies, plastic plates, cups and cutlery, party hats, party bags, toy food, pieces of fruit, hoop, bean bags, birthday cards, playdough, skipping ropes, string, chalk

EXPLORE

Taking every opportunity throughout the school day to build and reinforce mathematical concepts gives children's learning purpose and meaning in the wider context of their lives.

ACTIVITY	AREA	DESCRIPTION	RESOURCES
Birthday party	Classroom	Set up items for children to role-play a birthday party. Use teddies so children can count out party hats or party bags and put up to 5 items in each bag.	Teddies, plates, cups, food, party hats, party bags
A table set for 5	Home corner	Children set the table for 5 people by counting out 5 plates, cups and a piece of fruit per plate.	5 plates, 5 cups, pieces of fruit
Bean bags in a hoop	Outside	Play a game with a hoop and 5 bean bags. Ask: *Can you throw the 5 bean bags into the hoop? How many bean bags did you get in the hoop?*	Hoop, 5 bean bags

Unit 1: Numbers to 5, Week 3: Counting to 5

Day 1

Learning focus

Stable order of counting to 5

Before you teach

- What resources will you provide to support children counting from a picture or with a rhyme?
- How will you provide scaffolding to help children relate amounts of concrete materials to abstract numerals?
- Consider how counting can be incorporated into daily routines to support children's learning.

Starter

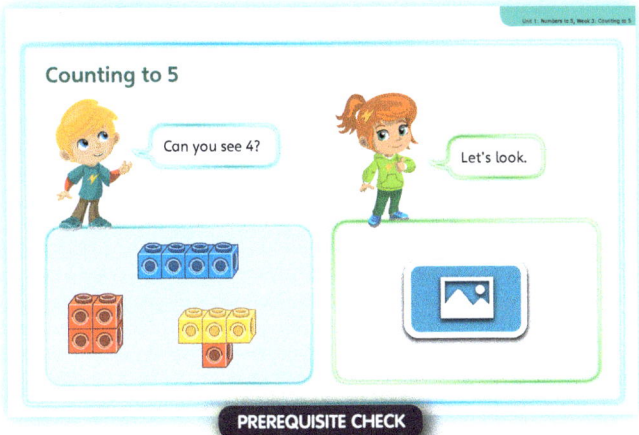

PREREQUISITE CHECK

PREREQUISITE CHECK Can children identify that all the models show 4, even though they are arranged differently?

WAYS OF WORKING Whole class
Where possible, give children access to cubes so that they can replicate the models on the **Online Flashcard**.

IN FOCUS This **Prerequisite check** practises the skill of reliably counting 4 objects. Children may be able to 'see' 4 (subitising) rather than having to count.

ASK
- *How many cubes are there? Does it matter that some of the cubes are different colours? Does it matter that some are shown in different shapes?*

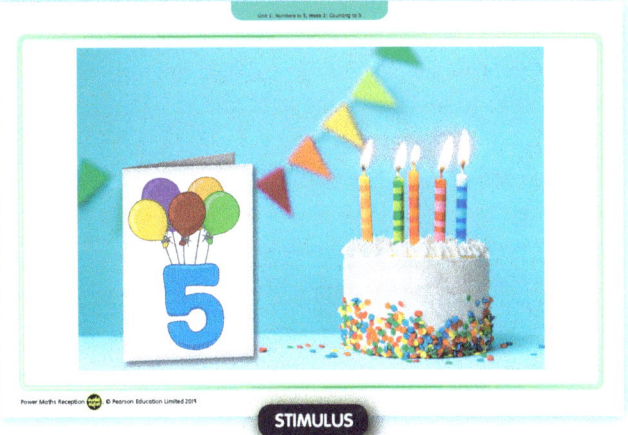

STIMULUS

STIMULUS Photograph prompting a guided activity
The photograph shows a birthday cake with 5 candles, and a birthday card with the number 5 on the front. Birthdays are a great context for introducing the concept of 5, as many children will be familiar with birthdays and many of them will be turning 5 during the year.

WAYS OF WORKING Whole class
Set up 5 teddies in a row with a birthday card in an envelope in the middle. Have a birthday cake, candles, party bags and party hats to help set the scene. Open the card and reveal that it is a 5th birthday card. Explain that you need to put enough candles on the cake for the teddy's birthday.

IN FOCUS The focus of this **Stimulus** is to build confidence in the one-to-one correspondence of counting to 5, using the rule of cardinality (that the last number you say is the total amount). Practise counting groups of objects up to 5 out loud to reinforce this.

ASK
- *What number is on the card? Who else is 5? Is anyone going to be 5 soon?*
- *How many candles do you need for the cake? Can you count them out?*
- *Can you show me how many candles you need on your fingers?*

GET ACTIVE Make playdough birthday cakes with children – one cake for each small group of children. Give each group a range of birthday cards with different numbers on them from 1–5. Children choose a card and put the correct number of candles on a playdough cake to match the card.

39

Unit 1: Numbers to 5, Week 3: Counting to 5

Day 2

Learning focus
One-to-one correspondence to 5

Discover

WAYS OF WORKING Whole class or small groups
Ensure candles and five frames are available to support counting.

IN FOCUS The focus of this **Discover** is to use the familiar 5th birthday party setting to give children many opportunities to see and count up to 5.

ASK
- How can you count the candles? Can you show me on your fingers?
- What else in the picture can you count? How many children (hats, balloons) are there?
- Can you see how many balloons there are, without counting each one?

STRENGTHEN Use 5 children or teddies to recreate the **Discover** picture. Encourage children to set the table for the party. Ask: *How many plates do you need? Can you count them out one by one?* Repeat with other items and count them out onto the table.

DEEPEN To extend thinking in this session, prompt children to look at the **Discover** picture again. Ask: *Are there enough balloons for each child? How could you find out?* Use 5 children or 5 teddies to represent children in the picture and match each balloon to a child.

Share

WAYS OF WORKING Whole class

IN FOCUS Children represent 5 using candles and use a five frame to scaffold their counting. Eventually children will make the link between a five frame and the amount 5, supporting their ability to 'see' an amount represented in the five frame without needing to count out every object.

ASK
- How does a five frame help you to count the candles?
- Can you fit any more candles in the five frame?

STRENGTHEN Use a five frame and real objects to represent the pictures. Encourage children to touch each item as they count. Ask children to count backwards from 5 using the items in the five frame.

DEEPEN Develop children's counting by asking them to count in specific orders. Show five candles where one is slightly different. Say: *This candle is our special candle.* Can children count the candles making the special one number three or number five? Ask: *Are there always 5 candles, no matter where the special one is placed? How do you know?* [The five frame is full, we have not taken any away or added any more.] *Count backwards starting with number 5.*

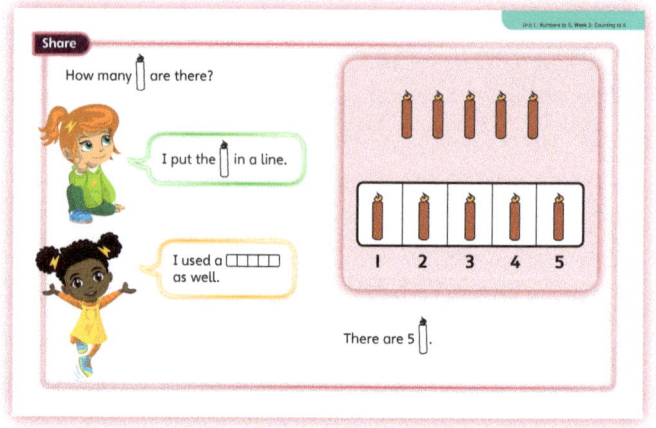

GET ACTIVE Give children a party bag each and ask them to find and count out up to 5 objects to put into the bag. Ask them to discuss with a partner which items they have chosen. Ask: *How do you know you have 5?* Ask some children to show the class what they put in their bag. Encourage everyone to count aloud as the objects are taken out of the bag.

Unit 1: Numbers to 5, Week 3: Counting to 5

Day 3

Learning focus
Order irrelevance to 5

Think together

WAYS OF WORKING Whole class or small groups
Ensure five frames and dice are available for this **Think together**. Ensure children are familiar with the five frame and how it is used before starting this session.

IN FOCUS The learning focus is order irrelevance, so concentrate on counting the candles (Question ❶) several times, starting with a different one each time to ensure that children understand that there are still 5. In Question ❷ the hats are displayed in the traditional dice formation for 5, encouraging children to 'see' 5 without counting, but check by starting at different places to count.

ASK
- Question ❶: *Can you say the number of candles out loud as you count? How many candles are there?*
- Question ❷: *How many hats are there? Which dice face has the same pattern? How does this help you to know how many hats there are?*

STRENGTHEN Make a large five frame on the floor using skipping ropes or string. Using 5 plates – 4 that are the same colour or size and 1 that is different – encourage children to count out the plates into the five frame making

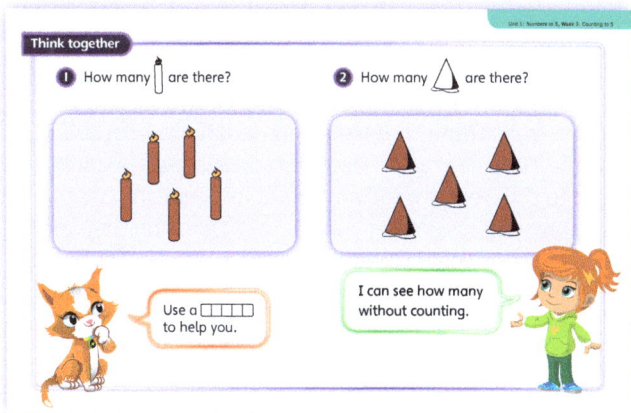

the 'different plate' a different number in the count each time. Ask: *Can you make this plate number 3 in the count? Now make it number 4.*

DEEPEN Use the **Multilink cube teaching tool** to show cubes in traditional dice arrangements and the **Five frames teaching tool** to show different arrangements on a five frame. Can children show how many by holding up the same number on their fingers? This activity encourages children to recognise representations of numbers to 5, without having to count each item every time.

Practice: Journal 1

WAYS OF WORKING Independent thinking

IN FOCUS The first part of the **Practice** activity focuses on the five frame, showing examples of 3, 4 and 5. Draw children's attention to the empty cells in the five frame for 3 and 4 and that for 5 it is full. The second part encourages children to begin subitising (identifying an amount by looking at it, rather than needing to count each item). Allow them to build the models using 5 multilink cubes.

MASTERY CHECKPOINT Look at the different ways that children represent 5. Can they count out 5 each time or do they move the cubes they have counted out, understanding that the number does not change even though it is in a different arrangement? Can any children subitise without needing to count out each cube?

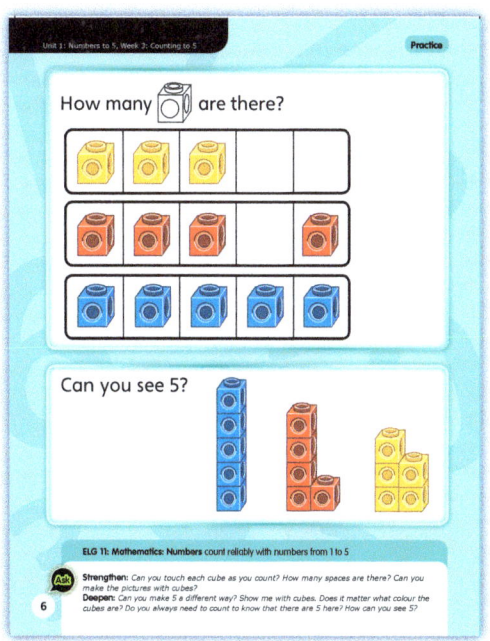

Unit 1: Numbers to 5, Week 3: Counting to 5

Day 4

Learning focus
Representations of 5

Challenge

WAYS OF WORKING Whole class or small groups
Prepare a range of resources for this session, including cubes and five frames. For any children still mastering the learning from **Think together**, choose different objects from the classroom and place them on a large five frame. Model to children how moving the objects doesn't change how many objects there are altogether. Question them on this as you carry out the activity to stimulate their thinking.

IN FOCUS The focus of this **Challenge** activity is to count numbers up to and including 5 in different formations, to ensure that children are really secure with counting to 5. The variation in this **Challenge** helps to address the misconception that 5 is only 5 if it is presented in a certain way, and should help to identify children who need further support with this concept. Children need to be confident counting to 5, however it is represented.

ASK
- Which of the pictures shows 5? Which picture does not show 5? How do you know?
- Can you use cubes to make each image yourself?

STRENGTHEN Create a giant five frame for children to stand in (using chalk, string or skipping ropes). Ask 2 children to stand in it. Move children around in the frame, asking each time: How many are there now? Repeat with 3, 4 or 5 children, varying their positions in the five frame. It is vital that children see the order irrelevance here, so keep asking them how many and how they know.

DEEPEN Use the **Five frame teaching tool** and place 1, 2, 3, 4 or 5 counters into the five frame. Display the five frame just long enough for children to count how many, then hide it on the screen. Ask children to recreate what they saw on individual five frames.

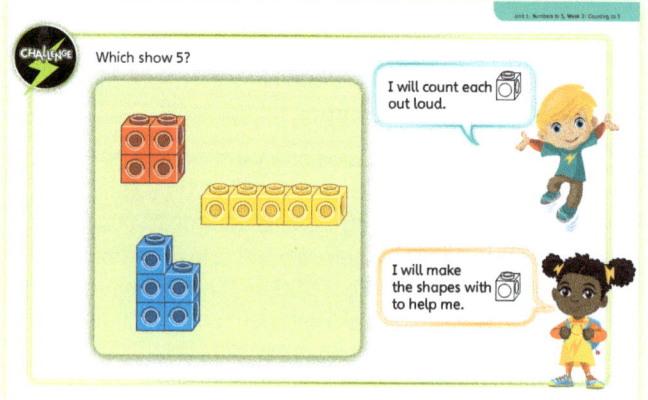

Unit 1: Numbers to 5, Week 3: Counting to 5

Day 5

Learning focus

Counting to 5 using abstraction

Practical activities

WAYS OF WORKING Whole class or small groups

IN FOCUS These activities build on children's understanding of counting to 5, by counting something abstract (something they cannot see). This is an important next step in their understanding of 5.

GET ACTIVE How many claps?

Explain that you are going to clap up to 5 times and that you want children to show, on their fingers, how many claps they heard. Ask children to close their eyes. Clap up to 5 times. Repeat, varying the number of claps.

Pass the parcel

Prepare a game of pass the parcel where each layer reveals an instruction or picture clue to do something to demonstrate children's understanding of numbers up to 5: jump 4 times, clap 5 times, spin 3 times, hop 5 times. Children may need help reading the instructions, but ask them to read the numerals themselves.

Reflect: Journal 2

WAYS OF WORKING Independent thinking

IN FOCUS Children **Reflect** on their learning by drawing a picture of a '5 party'. This could include a variety of pictorial representations of 5, such as 5 balloons, 5 candles, 5 plates, 5 party hats. Use the **Strengthen** prompts on the journal page to support children who need help getting started. Use the **Deepen** prompts to extend and challenge the thinking of children who complete this activity with little support.

MASTERY CHECKPOINT **Children who have mastered this concept** can confidently count up to 5 and can recognise and represent 5, following models that have been covered in the lesson.

Children who have not yet mastered this concept can recognise 5, but cannot necessarily recreate it themselves without support.

Children who have mastered this concept with greater depth can confidently count up to 5 and backwards from 5 to 1. They can recreate 5 in a variety of ways.

Unit 2
Sorting

Mastery Expert tip! "Noticing similarities and differences is an important part of being mathematical. It is valuable for children to see that shapes and designs have many different characteristics and can be sorted in a variety of ways. Encourage mathematical talk, being descriptive, paying attention to detail and being specific. These are all mathematical skills that are valuable to develop. Allow children to be creative and create their own collections with a variety of characteristics."

Don't forget to watch the Exploring composition video!

ELGs

This unit supports the following ELGs:

→ **ELG 11: Mathematics: Numbers**
count reliably with numbers from 1 to 20, place them in order and say which number is one more or one less than a given number

→ **ELG 12: Mathematics: Shape, space and measures**
explore characteristics of everyday objects and shapes and use mathematical language to describe them

→ **ELG 14: Understanding the world: The world**
know about similarities and differences in relation to places, objects, materials and living things

WHY THIS UNIT IS IMPORTANT

This unit focuses on noticing similarities and differences in collections of objects found in the classroom. Children will have the opportunity to sort objects into two groups based on size, colour and shape. They will discover that collections can be sorted in a number of ways and into more than two groups.

WAYS OF WORKING

Where possible, provide real-life versions of the objects represented in the pictures for children to model the activity. Give children the opportunity to discuss the similarities and differences between a pair of objects first, using a variety of criteria (colour, shape, size), then with 3 objects, where one is the same shape but a different colour to one of the others (1 red triangle, 1 yellow triangle, 1 red square). Ask children to find an object that is the same or different in some way as the one shown and to explain in what way it is different or the same.

WHERE THIS UNIT FITS

→ Unit 1: Numbers to 5
→ **Unit 2: Sorting**
→ Unit 3: Comparing groups within 5

In this unit, children will sort up to 5 objects into two or more groups using the size, colour or shape characteristics of the items being sorted.

Link to Key Stage 1

Number – number and place value
- count to and across 100, forwards and backwards, beginning with 0 or 1, or from any given number; count, read and write numbers to 100 in numerals; count in multiples of twos, fives and tens

Geometry – properties of shape
- recognise and name common 2D and 3D shapes, including: 2D shapes [for example, rectangles (including squares), circles and triangles]

This unit underpins the KS1 objectives for accurate counting using numbers to 5 and begins to explore that properties of shapes can be used to find similarities and differences.

Unit 2: Sorting

ASSESSING MASTERY

Children who have mastered this unit will be able to:
- sort up to 5 objects into two groups
- describe how they have sorted the objects
- know that there is often more than one way to sort a collection
- understand that a collection can be sorted into more than two groups

COMMON MISCONCEPTIONS	STRENGTHENING UNDERSTANDING	GOING DEEPER
Children may only notice the distinct groups when the objects are arranged into two clearly identifiable groups.	Give lots of opportunity for children to 'spot the difference' and 'spot the odd one out' in pictures. Start with groups of objects arranged in clear sets, then mix them up.	Explain **why** and in what way something is different or the same.
Children may sort objects by name rather than characteristics.	Give children plenty of opportunity to sort interesting collections using their own rules or criteria.	Give opportunity for mathematical talk about how each collection has been sorted and reasons for doing so.

STRUCTURES AND REPRESENTATIONS

Although there are no set mathematical structures and representations for this unit, different colour cubes, counters and 2D shapes may be useful for sorting. Sorting 2D shapes will provide the opportunity for children to become familiar with their properties.

RESOURCES

Mandatory: paintbrushes, glue spatulas, variety of objects from the classroom that can be sorted into groups based on physical characteristics of colour, size or shape: coloured counters in two different colours and sizes, crayons, pencils, toy vehicles

Optional: buttons, shells, various containers for sorting, balls, toy farmyard animals, labels, 2D shapes, washing up bowl

KEY LANGUAGE

There is some key language that children will need to know as part of the learning in this unit:
→ one, two, three, four, five, 1, 2, 3, 4, 5
→ sort, group, object
→ same, different, **odd one out**
→ size, shape, colour, pattern, triangle, square, bigger, smaller, counter, cube
→ how many, **more than**
→ describe, explain

Unit 2: Sorting, Week 4: Sorting into 2 groups

Sorting into 2 groups

Learning focus
This week, children will focus on similarities and differences in sets of objects found in the classroom. Children will sort objects into two groups based on size, colour and shape. They will discover that groups can be sorted in different ways and into more than two groups.

Small steps
→ Previous step: Counting to 5
→ **This step: Sorting into 2 groups**
→ Next step: Comparing quantities of identical objects

COMMON MISCONCEPTIONS
Children may only be able to spot the distinct groups when the objects are arranged into two clearly identifiable groups. Start with real objects in clear sets, discussing which are the same and which are different, then mix them up and repeat. Ask:
- *Which are the same? How are they the same? Which are different? How are they different?*

Children may sort objects by name rather than by characteristics. Use a variety of small sets of objects (2–5), varying the differences by colour, shape or size. Use sets of objects where the difference could be one of two characteristics, encouraging children to find both similarities and differences. For example: one yellow counter, one red counter, one red cube (colour or shape); one large and one small triangle, one large and one small square (shape or size). Ask:
- *What is the same? How are these objects the same? How are these objects different?*

KEY LANGUAGE
In lesson: one, two, three, four, five, 1, 2, 3, 4, 5, **sort**, **group**, **describe**, objects, how many, **more than**, same, different, **odd one out**

Other language to be used by the teacher: size, shape, colour, pattern, triangle, square, bigger, smaller, counter, cube, explain

RESOURCES
Mandatory: paintbrushes, glue spatulas, variety of objects from the classroom that can be sorted into groups based on physical characteristics (colour, shape or size) such crayons, pencils, toy vehicles

Optional: buttons, shells, 2D shapes, balls, toy farmyard animals, containers to sort objects into (baskets, pots or jars), labels, washing up bowl

EXPLORE
Taking every opportunity throughout the school day to build and reinforce mathematical concepts gives children's learning purpose and meaning in the wider context of their lives.

ACTIVITY	AREA	DESCRIPTION	RESOURCES
Button collection	Discovery table	Children sort buttons into groups and give rules to their groups (colour; number of holes; large or small).	Selection of buttons
Let's tidy up!	Classroom	Children sort resources around the classroom into clearly labelled baskets, boxes, trays or pots.	Containers, labels
Washing up	Art area	Children sort painting utensils into groups ready for washing up: brushes (large and small), glue spatulas, glue or paint pots.	Washing up bowl, painting utensils

Unit 2: Sorting, Week 4: Sorting into 2 groups

Day 1

Learning focus
What's the same and what's different?

Before you teach

- What objects will you provide for children to support their learning in this lesson?
- Can children describe the characteristics of a familiar object in terms of colour, pattern, shape and size?
- Are children familiar with the language 'same' and 'different'?

Starter

PREREQUISITE CHECK

PREREQUISITE CHECK Describing the football in terms of its physical characteristics.

WAYS OF WORKING Whole class
Encourage children to describe the various characteristics of the football in the image. If necessary, prompt them to describe the shape, colour, size and pattern of the ball.

IN FOCUS The **Prerequisite check** practises the language of description, encouraging children to observe the properties of an object.

ASK
- What words could you use to describe this object?

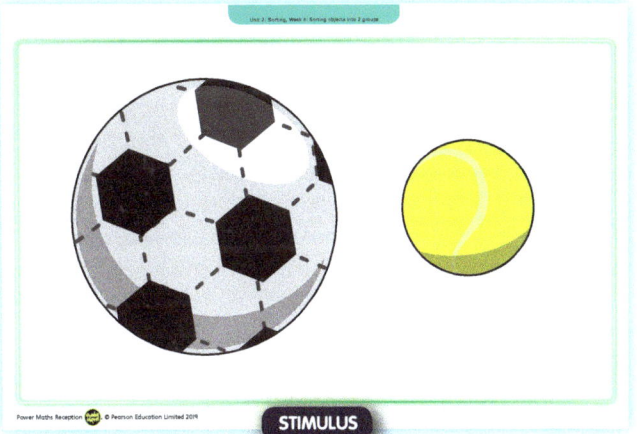

STIMULUS

STIMULUS Picture to prompt discussion
The picture of two different balls is intended to spark discussion about similarities and differences.

WAYS OF WORKING Whole class or in pairs
Encourage children to describe the physical characteristics of the football and the tennis ball and compare them in terms of what is the same and what is different. Prompt children to think about size, shape and colour.

IN FOCUS The focus is on practising the language of description and observing the properties of an object, using these observations to describe the similarities and differences between objects. This is an important foundation for being able to accurately sort a set of objects into groups.

ASK
- What is the same about these two objects?
- What is different about these two objects?
  What else is different about these two objects?

GET ACTIVE Ask children to find an interesting object in the classroom to share with a partner. Encourage children to describe what is the same and what is different about their objects. Encourage them to describe the shape, colour, pattern or size. Ask: *Are there any other similarities or differences?* Ask pairs of children to describe to the class what is the same and what is different about their two objects. Ask: *Who else has an object the same as X's? How is it the same? How is it different?* Children may struggle to notice that two very different objects can be 'the same' by virtue of their colour, shape or size. If appropriate, continue with identifying pairs of objects that have something the same and something different about them (large and yellow, small and yellow; used for art or one white, one red).

47

Unit 2: Sorting, Week 4: Sorting into 2 groups

Day 2

Learning focus

Sorting objects where there are two distinct groups

Discover

WAYS OF WORKING Whole class or small groups
Have real objects available for children to recreate the sorting activity.

IN FOCUS The focus of the **Discover** is to give children a familiar context from which to think about the concept of sorting. Tidying up equipment in the classrooms could be an activity they have not thought of as 'sorting' before. Placing this early mathematical concept in such a familiar context should give children more confidence to approach the task of sorting the paintbrushes and glue spatulas. Although the focus is sorting, build in opportunities for children to practise counting the objects, too.

ASK

- Can you spot something that has been put in the wrong place?
- How many paintbrushes are there? How many glue spatulas are there? How many things are in this jar altogether?
- How could you sort them? What could you sort the paintbrushes and glue spatulas into? [Demonstrate with real paintbrushes and glue spatulas and some empty jars if possible.]
- Are there any other objects in the picture that need sorting? How do you know? How could you sort them?

STRENGTHEN To support understanding of this sorting concept, set up a similar scene in the classroom. Muddle

glue spatulas and paintbrushes (or crayons and pens or two colours of paint pots) in a jar or basket and ask children to physically sort the objects into two jars or baskets. Encourage children to discuss what they are doing and why they are sorting as they are.

DEEPEN Ask children to sort the objects in the picture or on the table in a different way. For example, by colour or size rather than type. Can they sort the objects into more than two groups? Throughout the sorting process, encourage children to describe what they are doing out loud, to you or to a partner.

Share

WAYS OF WORKING Whole class

IN FOCUS The focus of **Share** is to demonstrate how the objects can be clearly sorted into two distinct groups. Placing all the objects from a group in a row gives children a strategy for helping them to sort if the groups are not, at first, immediately obvious. The jars in the picture are transparent so that children can see the objects inside in their entirety, using their physical features to inform how they sort.

ASK

- What does Dexter do to sort the objects? [Lays them all out first.] How does that help?
- Have the objects been sorted correctly? How do you know?

GET ACTIVE To embed learning, ask each child to find a collection of five small treasures from around the classroom, such as toy cars or animals, blocks, shells, cubes or buttons. Ask children to sort their collection into two groups. Depending on the treasures they have chosen, children may

need to be very creative with how they sort. Offer them a starting point by suggesting they first look at colour, then size. Are there any other physical features they can sort by? If they can't find a connection, allow children to swap one or two objects.

Unit 2: Sorting, Week 4: Sorting into 2 groups

Day 3

Learning focus

Discovering that there is more than one way to sort

Think together

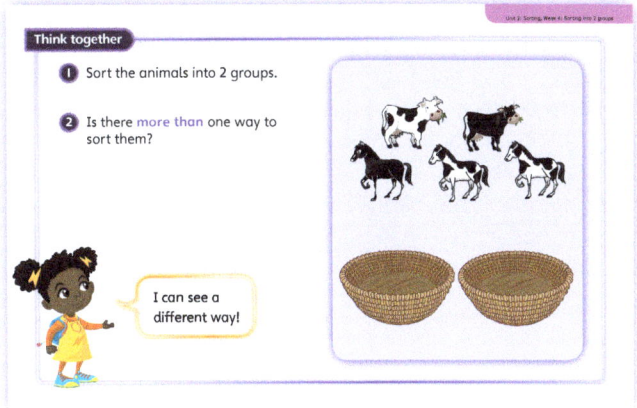

WAYS OF WORKING Whole class or small groups

IN FOCUS The focus of the **Think together** is to ask children to sort objects into two groups, guided by an image that gives them two clear ways to sort. Encourage children to discover the second way to sort for themselves by prompting them with Flo's statement: *I can see a different way!* Tease out the different methods of sorting by encouraging children to describe what is the same and what is different about the animals.

ASK

- Question ❶: *Which animals are shown in this picture? What do they look like? What is the same about the animals? What is different about the animals?*
- Question ❶: *How can you sort the animals into two groups?*
- Question ❷: *Is there another way to sort the animals into two groups?*
- Question ❷: *Can you sort the animals into more than two groups?*

STRENGTHEN Use every opportunity to strengthen and support understanding of how physical features can be used to sort groups of objects by modelling the key language of description when sorting. Ensure you are using the vocabulary *bigger, smaller, more, fewer, same, different*. Prompt children by encouraging them to look at colour, pattern, shape and size. If you have access to toy farmyard animals, set up similar groups of objects (up to 5) for children to sort and discuss – ensure the objects can be clearly sorted into two groups.

DEEPEN Give children who are secure sorting into two clearly defined groups opportunities to extend their thinking. Ask them to sort a given group of objects into more than two groups, or provide a group of objects to sort where there are two or three possible ways to sort them. Can they find all the ways to sort them? Can they find a group of objects (up to 5) for a partner to sort?

Practice: Journal 1

WAYS OF WORKING Independent thinking

IN FOCUS The focus of this **Practice** activity is to check that children can identify the groups. For the second part, check that children are familiar with the term *odd one out*. Ask: *What does it mean to be the odd one out? Can you use the words 'same' and 'different' to help you describe what this means?*

MASTERY CHECKPOINT Children who have mastered this concept can identify a group and discuss how the objects in the group could be sorted. Children can describe how the objects are the same or different, using the features of colour, size or shape. They can identify the object that is different, confidently using the term *odd one out*.

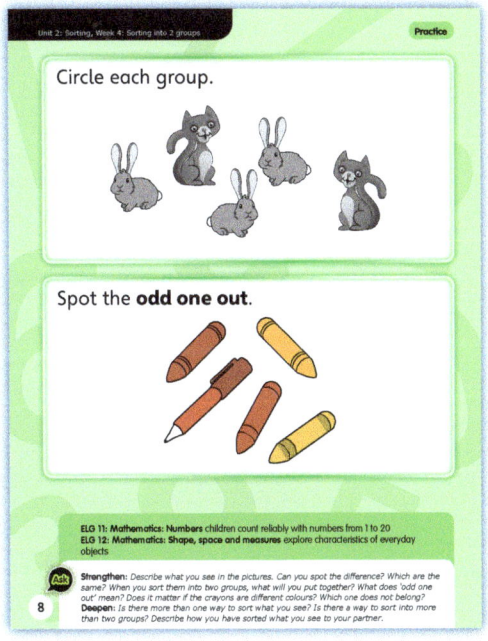

49

Day 4

Unit 2: Sorting, Week 4: Sorting into 2 groups

> **Learning focus**
> Sorting objects in more than one way

Challenge

WAYS OF WORKING Whole class or small groups

IN FOCUS This **Challenge** moves children on a step from **Think together** by asking them to think about all the ways the toys can be sorted. The options are: to sort by vehicle (one car, three vans, one bus), by size (one big, four small) or by colour (three red, two yellow with a blue stripe). Children who are not yet secure in their understanding of sorting to find all the possible ways should still be able to find and explain at least one way to sort these toys.

ASK
- How many toys are there? What sort of toys are they?
- What is the same and what is different about these toys?
- How could you sort these toys into two groups? Why have you sorted them like this?
- Do you think there is another way to sort the toys?
- How many different ways can you find to sort the toys?

STRENGTHEN For children who need more support and confidence when sorting, use physical resources from the classroom to recreate the picture in this activity. The act of physically moving the toys into groups will help children process and describe what they are doing and which characteristic they are using to sort the toys (size, shape, colour). Encourage children to draw how they have sorted the group as a way of recording what they have done, and then prompt them to think about another way to sort the objects. Each time they sort a different way, ask them to record their sorting with a drawing.

DEEPEN When children have found all the different ways, including three groups, encourage them to check, using counting to 5, that there are still 5 vehicles in each 'sort'. Some children may be able to write the numbers under each group. To extend thinking further for children who have demonstrated confidence in this activity give them a set of five 2D shapes to sort: two colours, two different shapes, two sizes. For example: one small yellow triangle, one small blue triangle, one small yellow circle, one small blue circle, one large blue circle or triangle; three cubes in two colours and two squares in the same two colours. Ask children to sort and record all the different ways these shapes can be sorted.

Unit 2: Sorting, Week 4: Sorting into 2 groups

Day 5

Learning focus
Sorting collections of objects

Practical activities

WAYS OF WORKING Whole class at start, then in pairs

IN FOCUS The focus of the activity is to give children confidence in sorting groups by asking them to collect their own group of objects (up to 5 objects in total) and then use the skills of description they have developed and practised in this unit to sort their objects.

GET ACTIVE Sorting collections

If possible, use the outside area to give children access to a variety of objects from nature that they can choose from to form their own 'collections'. Ask children to make a collection of 5 natural objects, such as leaves, stones, petals, shells. Working with a partner, can they sort their collections into two groups? Discussion is vital here: how have they sorted, why did they choose to sort their collections that way, is there a different way to sort their collections?

If children need a starting point, prompt them to look at the colour, pattern, shape and size of their objects. Give lots of positive feedback as they sort and then encourage one pair of children to share how they have sorted their collection with another pair of children. To finish off, move children inside and ask them to record how they have sorted their collections by drawing them in their groups.

Reflect: Journal 2

WAYS OF WORKING Independent thinking

IN FOCUS In this **Reflect** activity, children will reflect on their understanding of the concept of sorting by making their own collection of treasures using 5 objects from around the classroom or outside, and then sorting them in as many ways as they can. Allow children to swap one or two objects if they cannot find a way to sort them. Encourage children to describe how they have sorted their treasures and choose how to record this.

MASTERY CHECKPOINT **Children who have mastered this concept** can sort 5 objects into two groups and describe how they have sorted the objects.

Children who have not yet mastered this concept can describe one object in terms of its characteristics, for instance, its shape, size and colour but are not confident to sort a group of objects into two groups.

Children who have mastered this concept with greater depth can sort 5 objects into two or more groups and describe how they have sorted the objects. They know that there may be more than one way to sort a collection and that a collection can be sorted into more than two groups.

51

Unit 3
Comparing groups within 5

Mastery Expert tip! "Children need plenty of experiences where they can compare collections to talk about which group has more or fewer things. To begin with, focus on comparing familiar, identical objects, before moving on to familiar non-identical objects, to help children master and accurately apply the key vocabulary of *more*, *fewer* and *the same*."

Don't forget to watch the Comparing quantities video!

ELGs
This unit supports the following ELG:

→ **ELG 11: Mathematics: Numbers**
count reliably with numbers from 1 to 20, place them in order and say which number is one more or one less than a given number

WHY THIS UNIT IS IMPORTANT
This unit focuses on comparing two groups of objects and correctly identifying which has more, fewer or whether they have the same amount, using matching, representing and subitising strategies.

WAYS OF WORKING
Work as a whole class, in small groups or in pairs, as appropriate. Have countable objects and cubes available for children to use throughout this unit.

WHERE THIS UNIT FITS
→ Unit 2: Sorting
→ **Unit 3: Comparing groups within 5**
→ Unit 4: Change within 5

In this unit, children will be introduced to the language of *more* and *fewer* by comparing groups of up to 5 objects presented in different ways, including dice formation. They will also learn that groups of objects can have the same amount in them, even if they look different.

Link to Key Stage 1

Number – number and place value
- count to and across 100, forwards and backwards, beginning with 0 or 1, or from any given number; count, read and write numbers to 100 in numerals; count in multiples of twos, fives and tens
- identify and represent numbers using objects and pictorial representations including the number line, and use the language of: equal to, more than, less than (fewer), most, least

Unit 3: Comparing groups within 5

ASSESSING MASTERY

Children who have mastered this unit will be able to:
- identify if a group has more or fewer objects: they can line up objects to check which group has more or fewer; they can say if groups are equal; given an amount, they can show more or fewer with support
- compare two groups of non-identical objects and match them in order to find out which group has more, fewer or the same

COMMON MISCONCEPTIONS	STRENGTHENING UNDERSTANDING	GOING DEEPER
Children may not understand that *more* refers to the actual number of objects in the group rather than the size of the objects or the space they take up.	Count a group of two differently sized objects to ascertain that there are more of the smaller objects. Spread out the larger objects to take up more space or make a longer line and move the smaller objects close together. Count again to compare.	Put out a group of up to 4 larger objects and ask children to show you *more* using smaller objects. Repeat with smaller objects, asking children to show you *fewer* of a larger object.
Children may think that to compare two groups, one group must either be *more* or *fewer*, and cannot be *equal* or *the same*.	Show children pairs of the same number of objects (1–5), arranged differently. So, for example, 4 in a dice formation and in a horizontal line. Discuss what is the same and what is different to ascertain that one is not more than the other but the same.	In pairs, ask children to each show you the 'same but different': the same number of objects but arranged differently. They check that their partner has the same number in each group.

STRUCTURES AND REPRESENTATIONS

Multilink cubes: Multilink cubes provide a physical representation of an amount, which children can handle and move as they count to support their early counting skills.

Five frame: Five frames help to give children a sense of number, and support their understanding of number bonds to 5.

RESOURCES

Mandatory: multilink cubes, selection of countable real-life objects

Optional: number tracks, conkers, buckets (for sorting and grouping), flashcards showing representations of 5 in different arrangements (photocopiable 8), fruit bowls, selection of fruit, bikes, parking spaces, bags, plates, cups, cutlery, napkins, fruit, fruit skewers, containers for collecting objects, small objects for counting, five frame (photocopiable 7)

TEACHING TOOLS

multilink cubes

KEY LANGUAGE

There is some key language that children will need to know as part of the learning in this unit:
→ one, two, three, four, five, 1, 2, 3, 4 5
→ **more**, **fewer**, same, different, every
→ count, represent, match, sort, compare
→ equal, less than, fewer than, greater than, more than, equal amount

Unit 3: Comparing groups within 5, Week 5: Comparing quantities of identical objects

Comparing quantities of identical objects

Learning focus
This week, children will compare groups of identical objects using the language *more*, *fewer* and *less*. Identical objects are compared in different orientations, and include equal-quantity groups to prompt more creative thinking about how identical groups can be compared.

Small steps
→ Previous step: Sorting into 2 groups
→ **This step: Comparing quantities of identical objects**
→ Next step: Comparing quantities of non-identical objects

COMMON MISCONCEPTIONS

Children may miscount the objects and so compare the groups inaccurately. Ask:
- *What could you use to help you count the objects? How can you check your count?*

Children may think that a longer line of objects is a greater number of objects, even if they are not spaced evenly. Ask:
- *Can you line up the objects? Can you draw lines between them to match them one to one?*

KEY LANGUAGE

In lesson: one, two, three, four, five, 1, 2, 3, 4 5, **more**, **fewer**, counting/counted

Other language to be used by the teacher: represent, match, sort, compare, count, equal, less than, fewer than, greater than, more than, same, different

STRUCTURES AND REPRESENTATIONS

multilink cubes

RESOURCES

Mandatory: multilink cubes, selection of countable real life objects

Optional: number tracks, conkers, buckets (for sorting and grouping), flashcards showing representations of 5 in different arrangements (photocopiable 8), fruit bowls, selection of fruit, bikes, parking spaces, bags

EXPLORE

Taking every opportunity throughout the school day to build and reinforce mathematical concepts gives children's learning purpose and meaning in the wider context of their lives.

ACTIVITY	AREA	DESCRIPTION	RESOURCES
Comparing fruit	Snack area	Put some of the same fruits in two fruit bowls. Ask: *Which bowl has more bananas [or apples or oranges]?* Encourage children to estimate first before lining the fruit up to check.	Two fruit bowls, selection of fruit
Comparing children	Hall or classroom	Arrange children to sit in two rows. Ask: *Are there more children in the front row or the second row? Can you check by lining up?*	Children
Comparing bikes	Outside	Make 5 parking spaces for some bikes. Before tidying up, ask: *Are there more bikes in the parking spaces or in the playground? How can you check?*	Bikes, parking spaces

Unit 3: Comparing groups within 5, Week 5: Comparing quantities of identical objects

Day 1

Learning focus
Noticing inequality of groups

Before you teach
- Are children confident counting to 5?
- What resources and representations will you make available from previous lessons to support children's learning?

Starter

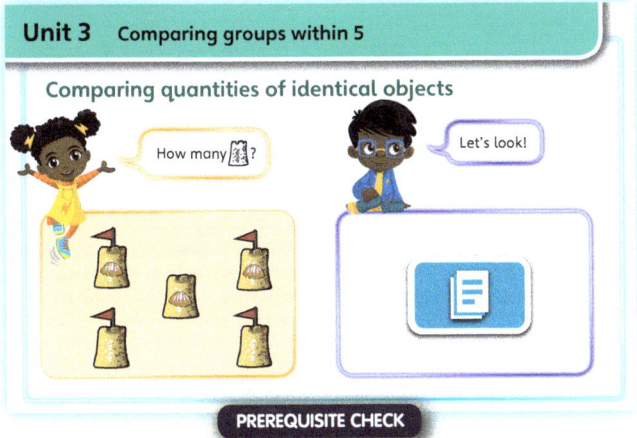

PREREQUISITE CHECK

STIMULUS

PREREQUISITE CHECK Picture of 5 sandcastles, some with flags, some with shells, some with both.

WAYS OF WORKING Whole class

IN FOCUS This **Prerequisite check** practises the Unit 1 skill of counting to 5 accurately and the Unit 2 skill of describing and sorting objects.

ASK
- Can you remember how to count to 5?
- How many sandcastles have flags?
- How many sandcastles have shells and flags?
- How many sandcastles have a shell and no flag?
- How many sandcastles are there altogether?

STIMULUS Photograph prompting a guided activity

WAYS OF WORKING Whole class

IN FOCUS The **Stimulus** introduces the idea of spotting differences between two similar images and introduces children to the questions: *What's the same?* and *What's different?*, prompting children to make comparisons. They could talk about the colour of the flowers, the shape of the vases or the number of flowers in each.

ASK
- What is the same about the vases/flowers?
- What is different about the flowers/vases?
- How many flowers can you see in each vase?

GET ACTIVE Create a picture using one type of countable objects, such as pebbles. Children start by copying the picture exactly. Children then try to make a picture that is different. Ensure children are always using the same object. As with the **Stimulus** photograph, use the **Ask** questions to guide discussion about what is the same and what is different.

Unit 3: Comparing groups within 5, Week 5: Comparing quantities of identical objects

Day 2

Learning focus

Comparing groups using more and fewer

Discover

WAYS OF WORKING Whole class or small groups
Ensure cubes or conkers, or objects to represent the conkers are available for children to use.

IN FOCUS Children count the items they can see in each picture and compare the groups using the language *more* and *fewer*. They can recreate the lines showing the conkers. Discuss and demonstrate, where necessary, the importance of starting both lines at the same place (you could use a ruler as a baseline) and of keeping the first, second and third conkers in each line level with each other.

ASK

- How many conkers does each child have?
- Who has more? How many more do they have? How do you know?
- Can you compare the flowers? What else can you compare?

Share

WAYS OF WORKING Whole class
Children recreate the pictures using objects.

IN FOCUS Children represent the conkers using cubes in order to compare the quantities. This is the first time that children are shown how a concrete object (a cube) can be used to represent something (a conker). Using the questions below as a prompt, ensure that children are comfortable with this representation. A baseline is shown under the cubes to illustrate the importance of lining objects up when comparing them.

ASK

- What does a cube represent?
- How many cubes do you need to represent Ella's conkers? How many cubes do you need to represent Tom's conkers?
- Why have you lined up the cubes? Who has more conkers?

STRENGTHEN If children do not understand how a cube can represent an object (conker), use actual conkers to support them in their understanding. When the conkers are in the correct position, replace each conker with a cube, one at a time. If necessary, use five frames or number tracks to enable children to space the cubes equally.

DEEPEN Deepen children's thinking by showing them examples where items are not spaced out evenly so that

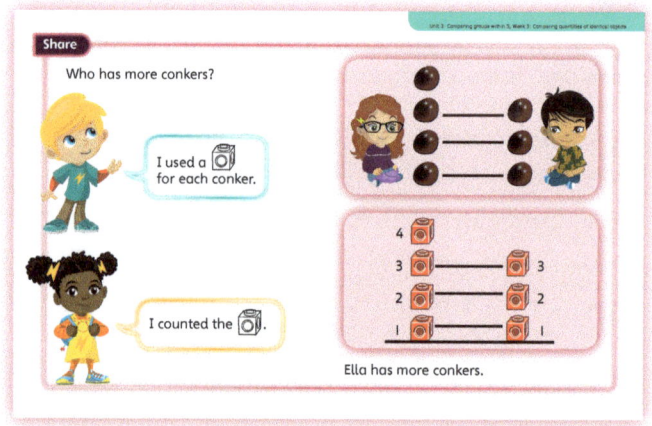

the smaller quantity looks as if it is more than the larger quantity. Challenge children to explain why this is not the case and to correct the problem by lining the objects up.

GET ACTIVE Provide children with two bags of identical objects (different amounts, up to 5). Challenge them to find out which bag has more. Children empty the contents of the bags and line up the objects inside, finding out which bag has more. Children can then create their own bags to challenge other children to find out which bag has more.

Unit 3: Comparing groups within 5, Week 5: Comparing quantities of identical objects

Day 3

Learning focus

Identifying more and fewer in different representations

Think together

WAYS OF WORKING Whole class

Ensure cubes are available for children to use.

IN FOCUS Children are introduced to the word *fewer* and use it to compare two groups. Prompt children to see that the same method of lining up the groups will still work to compare them. Question ❶ moves children on from **Share** by focusing on the concept of fewer as the opposite of more. Question ❷ moves children on a step further by varying the orientation of the lines of conkers. Children now think about how they can apply the same method of comparison to this new layout.

ASK

- Question ❶: *How many conkers does each child have?*
- Question ❶: *Who has fewer conkers? Who has more conkers? How do you know without counting?*
- Question ❷: Refer children to what Astrid is saying: *Can you see which is the longer line of conkers, without counting them? Will the longer line always be more?* [Only if the objects in both lines are spaced out equally.]
- Question ❷: *What's different about the conkers now?* [Changed to horizontal lines.]

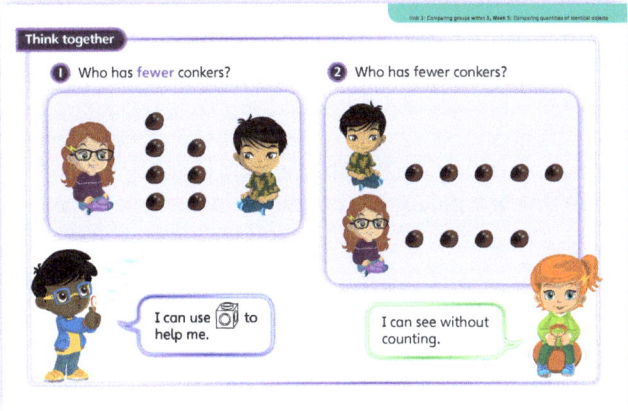

STRENGTHEN Provide children with two bags of identical objects (different amounts, up to 5). Give children a five frame each and encourage them to line up the objects, asking them to work out which bag has fewer. Can they use the five frame to show the different layouts in Questions ❶ and ❷?

DEEPEN Show children a bag containing 4 identical items. Show them another bag and explain that this bag has fewer inside it. Ask: *How many items could there be in the bag? How do you know?*

Practice: Journal 1

WAYS OF WORKING Independent thinking

IN FOCUS Children use their understanding of the language *more* and *fewer* to identify which character has more apples. Encourage children to justify their choice. Can they draw a child with fewer apples than Tom?

MASTERY CHECKPOINT Children who have mastered this concept can correctly identify the group that has more or fewer objects.

57

Unit 3: Comparing groups within 5, Week 5: Comparing quantities of identical objects

Day 4

Learning focus

Realising that quantities can be equal

Challenge

WAYS OF WORKING Whole class or in pairs
Use cubes or real-life objects to support learning.

IN FOCUS This activity focuses on comparing two groups that are equal. Children can either subitise that the amount of conkers are the same or line them up to check. Children realise that two groups can be equal and one group does not have to be more or fewer.

ASK

- How many conkers does each child have?
- How did you count the conkers? Can you line them up?
- Can you use the words more or fewer to describe the groups? What words **can** you use?

STRENGTHEN Make an amount using cubes or real-life objects, using the dice formation or similar. Ask children to make the same size group as you. Prompt children to match up the items in vertical or horizontal lines to show that the number in each group is equal.

DEEPEN Show representations of numbers up to 5 in different arrangements on the **Multilink cubes teaching tool** or on flashcards (photocopiable 8). Children make the same number using counters or cubes in a straight line to show an equal amount.

GET ACTIVE Give children buckets with images of up to 5 conkers on the front of each. Children collect the same number of conkers that they can see on the front of their bucket. Choose two buckets and ask children to compare the amount of conkers in each bucket, including two buckets containing the same amounts.

Unit 3: Comparing groups within 5, Week 5: Comparing quantities of identical objects

Day 5

Learning focus

Finding something that has more or fewer

Practical activities

WAYS OF WORKING Whole class

IN FOCUS These **Practical activities** build on children's understanding of more and fewer by finding more, fewer, or the same as something abstract. Children are given quantities and use them to find more or fewer.

GET ACTIVE **More, fewer or the same**

Clap three times. Ask: *Can you clap more times than me?* Hop four times. Ask: *Can you hop fewer times than me? Can you find more dice than I have? Can you find fewer cubes than I have? Can you find the same number of conkers as I have?* Repeat with a child doing an action up to 4 times and asking the other children to repeat with fewer, more or the same number.

Find the flashcard

Enlarge copies of the Numbers to 5 flashcards (photocopiable 8) and display around the classroom or outdoor area. Hold up one of the flashcards and call out *more*, *fewer* or *the same* and children run to a relevant flashcard.

Reflect: Journal 2

WAYS OF WORKING Independent thinking

IN FOCUS Children demonstrate their understanding of finding more or fewer by showing a ladybird with more spots. Can they draw a ladybird with fewer spots?

MASTERY CHECKPOINT **Children who have mastered this concept** can identify if a group has more or fewer objects. They can line up objects to check which has more or fewer. They can say if groups are equal. Given an amount, they can show more or fewer with support.

Children who have not yet mastered this concept can identify if a group has more or fewer objects when groups are aligned.

Children who have mastered this concept with greater depth can line objects up to show if a group has more or fewer items. They can say if groups are equal. Given an amount, they can show more or fewer independently.

Unit 3: Comparing groups within 5, Week 6: Comparing quantities of non-identical objects

Comparing quantities of non-identical objects

Learning focus

This week, children will compare two groups of non-identical objects saying which group of objects has more, fewer or the same. Children will build on learning from the previous week, matching objects to compare quantities, but focusing on matching non-identical objects to draw out the misconception that objects must be the same to compare them.

Small steps

→ Previous step: Comparing quantities of identical objects
→ **This step: Comparing quantities of non-identical objects**
→ Next step: One more

COMMON MISCONCEPTIONS

Children may think that a small group of larger objects will be more than a larger group of small objects. Ask:
- *Which group has more? Why do you think there are more in this group? How can you check which group has more?*

Children may think that objects must be identical in order to compare them. Ask:
- *How many (cups) are there altogether? How many cups are needed for 4 children? Does it matter if they are not the same colour?*

Children may think that to compare two groups, one group must either have more or fewer, and cannot be equal or the same. Ask:
- *How many are in this group? How many are in this group? Is that the same number or different?*

KEY LANGUAGE

In lesson: more, fewer, same, every, counting

Other language to be used by the teacher: different, more than, fewer than, equal amount, compare

STRUCTURES AND REPRESENTATIONS

multilink cubes

RESOURCES

Mandatory: multilink cubes

Optional: plates, cups, cutlery, napkins, clear bags, fruit, fruit skewers, containers for collecting objects, small objects for collecting, five frame (photocopiable 7)

EXPLORE

Taking every opportunity throughout the school day to build and reinforce mathematical concepts gives children's learning purpose and meaning in the wider context of their lives.

ACTIVITY	AREA	DESCRIPTION	RESOURCES
Set the table	Home corner	Children set the table for a given number of children (up to 5). Have up to 5 plates, cups, sets of cutlery, napkins.	Plates, cups, cutlery, napkins
Equal bags	Snack area	There are 5 apples in one bag and 2 in another bag. Ask: *Can you make the bags equal?*	Clear bags, fruit
Comparing collections	Classroom	Collections for children to sort and compare, identifying where there is more, less, fewer or the same.	Collection of small objects (toys, gems etc.)

Unit 3: Comparing groups within 5, Week 6: Comparing quantities of non-identical objects

Day 1

Learning focus
Comparing groups

Before you teach
- Can children accurately count up to 5 objects?
- Do children understand *how many* in terms of numbers to 5?
- Do children understand that 5 is more than 4, 4 is more than 2, for example?

Starter

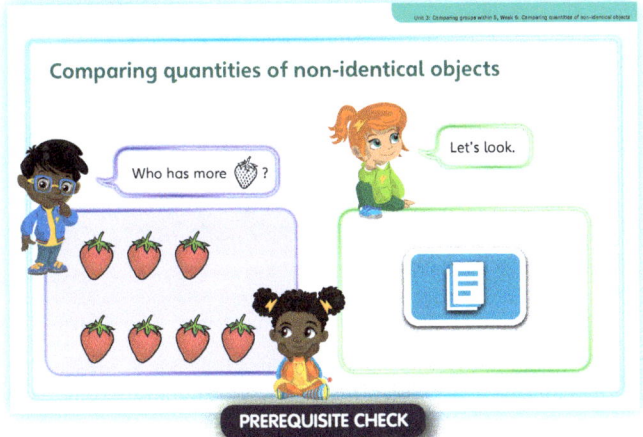

PREREQUISITE CHECK

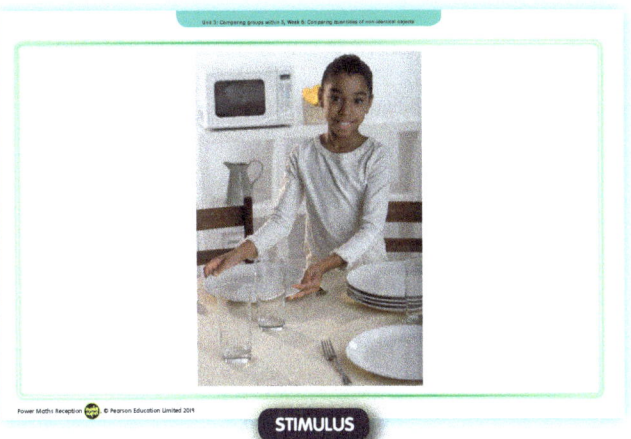

STIMULUS

PREREQUISITE CHECK Using the language *more* to compare two groups of identical objects.

WAYS OF WORKING Whole class

IN FOCUS This **Prerequisite check** practises the skill of comparing two groups of identical objects. Children can compare by looking, or can use cubes to represent the strawberries.

ASK
- How many strawberries does Ash have?
- How many strawberries does Flo have?
- Do you remember what 'more' means?
- Can you tell me who has more?

STIMULUS Photograph prompting a guided activity

WAYS OF WORKING Small groups

Using the photograph of a child helping to set the table as a stimulus for discussion, guide children towards a comparison of non-identical objects using the **Get Active** activity below.

IN FOCUS The focus of the **Stimulus** photograph and activity is to prompt understanding that one-to-one correspondence does not only apply to objects that are the same.

GET ACTIVE In small groups, ask children to seat 4 teddy bears at a table. Encourage children to set the table for snack time. Provide a pile of 5 plates and 3 cups for children to give out (you could expand the activity with forks, spoons, toy fruit). Each teddy needs a plate.

ASK
- Does every teddy have a plate?
- Are there more plates or more teddies?
- Each teddy also needs a cup. What's wrong? [Children should notice that one teddy doesn't have a cup.]
- Are there fewer teddies or fewer cups?
- Are there more plates or more cups?

61

Unit 3: Comparing groups within 5, Week 6: Comparing quantities of non-identical objects

Day 2

Learning focus

Comparing groups of non-identical objects using one-to-one correspondence

Discover

WAYS OF WORKING Whole class or small groups
Ensure cubes are available for children to use to represent objects for comparison.

IN FOCUS The focus of the **Discover** is to start to compare two groups of objects where the items are not identical, but are the same size, and to begin to line up objects in two parallel lines in order to accurately match and then compare them. Children should be encouraged to match groups of objects as a strategy for comparison, and can practise representing objects with cubes, a core skill introduced in Week 5.

ASK
- How many oranges are there? How many apples are there?
- Can you say what 'more' means?
- How could you work out which fruit there are more of?

STRENGTHEN Children need lots of experiences where they can compare collections and begin to talk about which group has more items. Initially, the groups should be very obviously different, with one group having many more things than the other group. Include collections with items

that are different but similar in size (such as apples and oranges) to help develop the skill of visual comparison. The more difficult skill of comparing objects of different sizes will be introduced in a later unit.

DEEPEN Point out other groups of non-identical objects for comparison in the **Discover** picture, such as the plates and cups. Encourage children to compare these groups using similar questions to those in **Ask**.

Share

WAYS OF WORKING Whole class
Provide cubes and/or toy fruit to recreate the focus items from the **Discover** picture.

IN FOCUS The focus of **Share** is for children to begin matching in order to compare two groups of non-identical objects. Children need to have an understanding of the meaning of the word *matching* and how this can help to compare two groups of objects, identifying when there are more, fewer or the same.

ASK
- Refer children to what Ash is saying. *What can you use to represent the oranges and apples?*
- *How can you line them up or match them up to help you compare?*
- *Can you see which fruit there are more of? How do you know?*

STRENGTHEN Use the real fruits or a five frame and cubes to represent the fruits in the picture.

DEEPEN To extend thinking, use the classroom environment to sort and match non-identical objects such as pencils and felt-tip pens. Prompt children to line up and match their

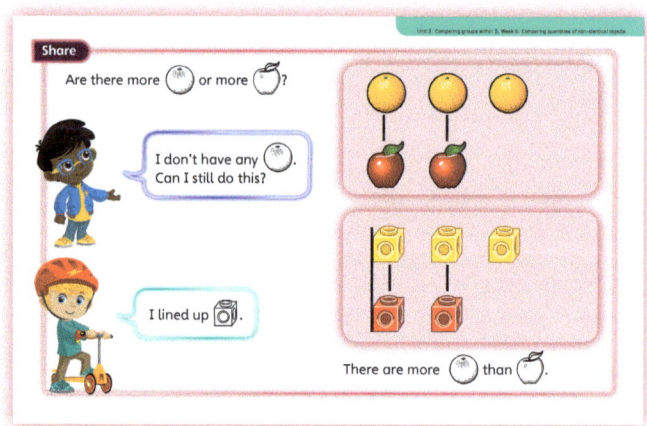

groups. Ask: *Which group has more? Which group has fewer? How can you check?*

GET ACTIVE Give children collections of cubes in two colours for them to put into parallel lines to compare. Ask: *Are there more red or more yellow cubes?*

Unit 3: Comparing groups within 5, Week 6: Comparing quantities of non-identical objects

Day 3

Learning focus

Comparing groups by matching or subitising

Think together

WAYS OF WORKING Whole class

IN FOCUS The focus of the **Think together** is to practise the skill of comparing non-identical objects by matching them in lines, as modelled in **Share**. The small step of progression between Question ① and Question ② is the comparison of *fewer* rather than *more*, and that the objects in Question ② are not aligned. Check that children understand the word fewer before attempting Question ②.

ASK

- Question ①: *How can you compare the purple plates and the green plates? Which group has more? How can you check?*
- Question ②: *What does 'fewer' mean? Can you see which group has fewer, without counting? How can you check?*

STRENGTHEN Encourage children to develop efficient comparing strategies by prompting them to decide what to do first. Ideally they should sort objects for comparison into two groups and then match them together, leading to a discussion about which has *more*, *fewer* or *an equal* amount.

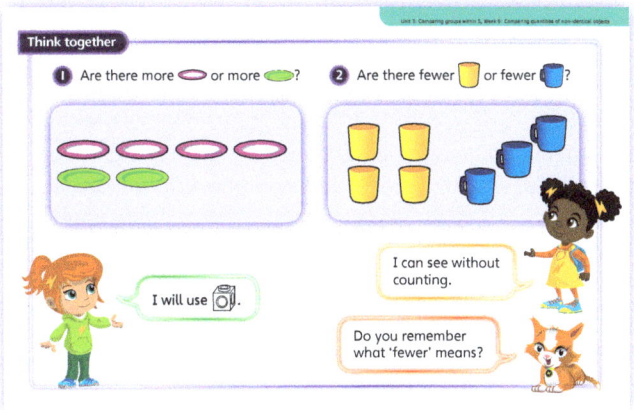

DEEPEN Challenge children to compare two non-identical groups without matching, but rather by seeing (subitising). Set up two groups of similarly sized non-identical objects (such as fruit, toy vehicles or animals) in familiar patterns (dice formations). Ask children to say which group has *more*, *fewer* or the *same* by looking, not counting or matching.

Practice: Journal 1

WAYS OF WORKING Independent thinking

IN FOCUS Children will need to decide how to work out the answer. The apples and oranges are presented in two parallel lines prompting children to draw lines to match them up. In the second part, the two groups of objects are displayed in familiar formations, encouraging children to see (subitise) which group has fewer.

MASTERY CHECKPOINT Children who have mastered this concept can sort and match non-identical objects into two groups in order to identify which group has more, fewer or the same. Children can subitise (where groups are displayed in familiar patterns) to accurately compare, without the need to match or count.

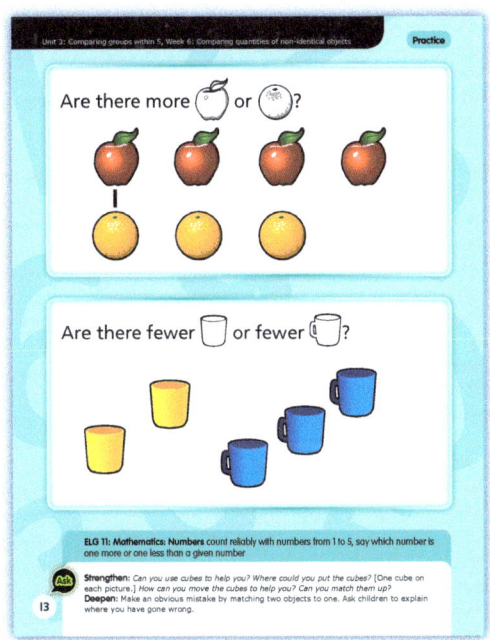

Unit 3: Comparing groups within 5, Week 6: Comparing quantities of non-identical objects

Day 4

Learning focus
Representing groups to compare using cubes

Challenge

WAYS OF WORKING Whole class or in pairs

Provide cubes for children to use to represent the objects.

IN FOCUS The focus of this **Challenge** is to apply the skill of matching to a new type of question. Children first need to work out that this is a comparison question, and then choose a strategy to help them make the comparison. The strawberries are in an irregular arrangement, so it is more difficult to see which group has more. Children apply the methods of representing objects with cubes and then matching them, as prompted by Astrid.

ASK
- *What do you need to do to answer this question?* [Make a comparison.]
- *How could you work this out?*
- Refer to what Astrid is saying: *Can you use cubes to help you? How?*
- *What should you do first? What should you do next?*
- *How can you check your answer?*

STRENGTHEN For children who have not yet acheived mastery, use real skewers and strawberries in the same quantities as the **Challenge**. Guide children to unpick the question by asking them to first line up the skewers and then line up the strawberries underneath. Ask: *Is this still a comparison question? How do you know? Show me how you can compare the skewers and the strawberries.*

GET ACTIVE Provide wooden skewers and a selection of fruit (larger fruits can be cut up into pieces). Make fruit skewers with children, leaving some pieces of fruit spare. Compare some of the skewers, ask: *Which one has more fruit pieces on it? Which one has fewer fruit pieces on it? Are there enough strawberries left over for each skewer to have another strawberry?*

DEEPEN Deepen understanding by taking opportunities to ask children to compare groups in everyday situations. For example, ask: *Are there more children in the reading corner or at the sand tray? Can every bowl have a spoon? Does every bike have a parking space?*

Unit 3: Comparing groups within 5, Week 6: Comparing quantities of non-identical objects

Day 5

Learning focus
Representing and comparing groups in a variety of ways

Practical activities

WAYS OF WORKING Whole class

IN FOCUS Working in the outside area, collect natural treasures. Children compare each other's collections, using the key mathematical vocabulary of *more*, *fewer* or *the same*.

GET ACTIVE **Natural object treasure hunt**
Give each child a bucket, basket or other container and ask them to go outside and find up to 5 natural objects each for a collection. When they have finished their treasure hunt, ask children to compare their collection with a partner. Whose collection has more or fewer, or are they the same? If helpful, ask children to empty their collection onto a table or the carpet and line it up under their partner's collection, to support their matching comparison. To extend the activity, ask children to swap partners and compare their collection with a different collection. Can they find a partner who has more, one who has less and one who has the same amount?

Reflect: Journal 2

WAYS OF WORKING Independent thinking

IN FOCUS Children decide how many more apples than oranges they will draw in their journals. To successfully complete this activity, children will need to be comfortable with their understanding of *more*, and then be able to transfer that understanding accurately onto the page.

MASTERY CHECKPOINT **Children who have mastered this concept** can compare two groups of non-identical objects and match them in order to find out which has more, fewer or the same.

Children who have not yet mastered this concept need support when comparing two groups of non-identical objects, rely on teacher support and matching to compare and are not confident using the terms *more*, *fewer* and *the same*.

Children who have mastered this concept with greater depth can compare two groups of non-identical objects using various strategies, including matching, representing and subitising. They are confident with the comparison language of *more*, *fewer* and *the same* and can apply this in various contexts.

65

Unit 4
Change within 5

Mastery Expert tip! "When teaching this unit I made sure that I modelled the mathematical language regularly to the children, asking them to say it back to me. This helped their understanding. They loved making up their own *first*, *then*, *now* stories about things that interested them and some of them even made up their own songs!"

Don't forget to watch the Comparing quantities video!

ELGs

This unit supports the following ELG:

→ **ELG 11: Mathematics: Numbers**
count reliably with numbers from 1 to 20, place them in order and say which number is one more or one less than a given number

WHY THIS UNIT IS IMPORTANT

This unit focuses on finding one more and one less than a number within 5. It lays the foundation for addition and subtraction although, at this stage, children should not be expected to use the addition or subtraction signs. It is important to introduce this concept in a real life context and allow children to practise through play.

WAYS OF WORKING

Ensure children have access to five frames and cubes throughout this unit. Cubes can be used to represent any objects and different colours are useful when finding one more. By connecting the cubes together, children can see that the *whole* has changed. Give children opportunities to work together but also independently to check if they have fully understood the concept for themselves.

WHERE THIS UNIT FITS

→ Unit 3: Comparing groups within 5
→ **Unit 4: Change within 5**
→ Unit 5: Time

In this unit, children will learn how to find one more and one less than a number within 5 in the context of a *first*, *then*, *now* story structure. They will use pictures, objects and a five frame to show what is happening.

Link to Key Stage 1

Number – number and place value

- count to and across 100, forwards and backwards, beginning with 0 or 1, or from any given number; count, read and write numbers to 100 in numerals; count in multiples of twos, fives and tens
- given a number, identify one more and one less
- identify and represent numbers using objects and pictorial representations including the number line, and use the language of: equal to, more than, less than (fewer), most, least

Measurement

- sequence events in chronological order using language [for example, before and after, next, first, today, yesterday, tomorrow, morning, afternoon and evening]

This unit underpins the KS1 objectives for accurate counting, forwards and backwards, and for identifying one more and one less than a number. It also introduces the ideas of representing numbers pictorially using a five frame and sequencing of events.

Unit 4: Change within 5

ASSESSING MASTERY

Children who have mastered this unit will be able to:
- find one more and one less than a number within 5, and demonstrate this using a five frame and cubes
- tell first, then, now stories to express one more or one less
- use the vocabulary *one less* and *one more* in the correct context

COMMON MISCONCEPTIONS	STRENGTHENING UNDERSTANDING	GOING DEEPER
Children may count incorrectly when finding one more. Children may see one more than 2 as 1, 2, 1 instead of 1, 2, 3.	Use first, then, now stories to show that the whole has changed from 2 to 3. Use multilink cubes to show that 1 has been physically added to 2 which makes the total now 3.	Expose children to the misconception and ask them to justify why the answer is 3 not 1.
Children may confuse one less with one more.	Use different coloured cubes to show one more; use crossing out to show one less. Do not use different coloured cubes for one less as this could lead to the misconception.	Explore one more than 0 and one less than 1.

STRUCTURES AND REPRESENTATIONS

Five frame: Five frames help to give children a sense of number, and support their understanding of one more and one less.

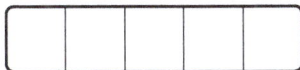

Multilink cubes: Multilink cubes provide a physical representation of an amount, which children can handle and move as they explore one more and one less.

RESOURCES

Mandatory: five frames (photocopiable 7), multilink cubes

Optional: small toys for counting, objects from nature, laminated print outs of numerals 1–5 (photocopiables 2–6), building blocks, pictures of towers, home corner items (plates, cups, chairs), washing line, pegs, socks, mini whiteboards

TEACHING TOOLS

five frame, multilink cubes

KEY LANGUAGE

There is some key language that children will need to know as part of the learning in this unit:
➔ one, two, three, four, five, 1, 2, 3, 4, 5, none, zero
➔ count, **forwards**, **backwards**, how many
➔ **first**, **then**, **now**
➔ **one less**, **one more**, **order,** fewer, take away, add, altogether
➔ number story, represent, five frame

Unit 4: Change within 5, Week 7: One more

One more

Learning focus

This week, children will learn about one more within 5. They will use role play and *first, then, now* story structures to explore adding one more. Children will learn to recognise that the next number they count is one more than the previous number.

Small steps

→ Previous step: Comparing quantities of non-identical objects
→ **This step: One more**
→ Next step: One less

COMMON MISCONCEPTIONS

When adding one more, children may see objects as two separate groups rather than a combined whole. Children may assume when adding one more that 1 is the answer because of the use of the word *one* in the question. The *first, then, now* story structure in this unit will address this misconception. Ask:
- *How many are there altogether? Can you count everything in the new group?*

When adding one more onto a five frame, children may think that where the item is placed will affect the answer. For example, they may think that if there are 2 cubes in the first 2 spaces of a five frame, and then one more is added to the fifth space, there are now 2 and 1 rather than 3. Ask:
- *Does it matter where you add this counter to the five frame? Will you still have one more if you put it here? What about if you put it here?*

KEY LANGUAGE

In lesson: one, two, three, four, five, 1, 2, 3, 4, 5, how many, represent, one more, first, then, now, order, five frame

Other language to be used by the teacher: number story, add, altogether, count

STRUCTURES AND REPRESENTATIONS

multilink cubes, five frames

RESOURCES

Mandatory: multilink cubes, five frames

Optional: small objects for counting, laminated print outs of numerals 1–5 (photocopiables 2–6), building blocks, pictures of towers made from blocks, home corner items (plates, cups, chairs), washing line, pegs, socks

EXPLORE

Taking every opportunity throughout the school day to build and reinforce mathematical concepts gives children's learning purpose and meaning in the wider context of their lives.

ACTIVITY	AREA	DESCRIPTION	RESOURCES
Set the table	Home corner	Set the table for 3 people then explain that one more person is coming for lunch so they need to set another place. Ask: *What else do you need? You need one more plate, one more cup, etc.*	Plates, cups, chairs, general home corner items
Find one more	Classroom	Children take a number then find things to make one more than their number.	Laminated print outs of numerals 1–5 (photocopiables 2–6)
Build a tower	Outdoor area	Have pictures of towers that are 2, 3 and 4 blocks tall. Challenge children to build a tower that is one block taller.	Blocks, pictures of towers

Unit 4: Change within 5, Week 7: One more

Day 1

Learning focus

Adding one more

Before you teach

- Are all children secure with one-to-one correspondence of numbers to 5?
- Can children count up to 5 objects accurately?
- Do children understand what the word *more* means?

Starter

PREREQUISITE CHECK

PREREQUISITE CHECK Counting 5 children

WAYS OF WORKING Whole class

IN FOCUS This **Prerequisite check** is designed to ensure that children are confident counting 5 items before starting to think about adding one more to an existing amount.

ASK

- *How can you count the children?*

STIMULUS

STIMULUS Photograph prompting a guided activity
Talk through what is happening in the photograph using the vocabulary of *first*, *then* and *now*. The child at the side is about to join in play so at *first* there are 2 children playing, *then* one more joins in, *now* there are 3 children playing.

WAYS OF WORKING Whole class

IN FOCUS This **Stimulus** is designed to prompt children to think about adding one more to an existing amount.

ASK

- *How many children are in the photo?*
- *How many children are playing?*
- *If this child joins in, how many will be playing now?*

GET ACTIVE Choose three children to demonstrate the activity. Ask two children to stand as a pair. Say: *First there are 2 children.* Then ask the third child to join the group. Say: *Then one more joins the group. Now there are 3 children.* Each time ask children to repeat the statement. Now put the sentence together and ask children to repeat it out loud: *First there are 2 children, then one more joins the group. Now there are 3 children.*

Put some children into groups of 3 and ask the remaining children to join one of these groups. Ask: *How many children are in the group now? Can you say a first, then, now sentence to describe what happened?* First there are … children, then … joined, now there are … children. In their groups, ask children to role-play the same situation using toys or objects. They should start with 2 or 3 objects and add one more, explaining what has happened using a first, then, now structure.

69

Day 2

Learning focus
Adding one more with number stories

Discover

WAYS OF WORKING Whole class or small groups

The **Discover** picture could be introduced practically in the outdoor area using parking bays and bikes. This can then be replicated using five frames and objects such as cars and cubes.

IN FOCUS This **Discover** activity focuses on exploring what happens when one more is added to an object or group of objects.

ASK
- How many bikes are in the first picture? Then what happens?
- How many bikes are in the 'now' picture?
- Can you say this as a first, then, now story? What is one more than 2?
- What do the parking bays look like? [a five frame]

STRENGTHEN Offer these stem sentences for children to complete: **First** there are … bikes, **then** …, **now** there are …. Encourage children to tell a partner a story about the pictures using this story structure.

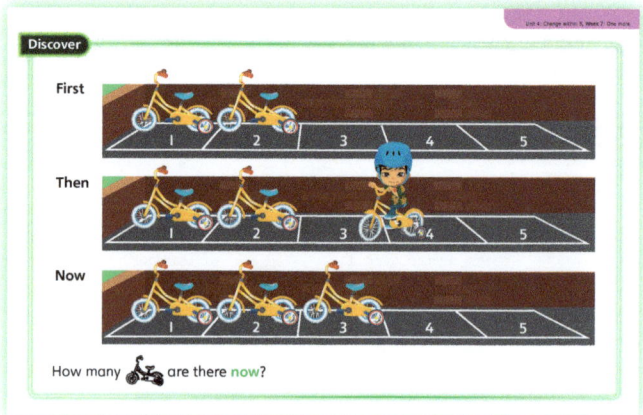

DEEPEN Hide different parts of the story to encourage children to recall the full story and use the language more independently. Some children may start to think about what happens when one more is added to 0.

Share

WAYS OF WORKING Whole class

Have cubes and five frames available for children to represent the story. The **Five frame teaching tool** can be used to replicate the **Share**.

IN FOCUS Links are made between the bikes, a concrete representation of the bikes in the bays (the cubes in a five frame) and the numbers. The use of cubes is encouraged to show children how they can represent objects using other objects. The arrow in the *then* image is key to show the change when adding more.

ASK
- How many cubes do you need to represent the first picture?
- How many more cubes are added? Can you show this on a five frame?
- Can you tell the story as you act it out?

STRENGTHEN Children should be encouraged to tell first, then, now stories out loud as much as possible. Give children opportunities to use real-life objects such as bikes or toy cars to physically act out the story.

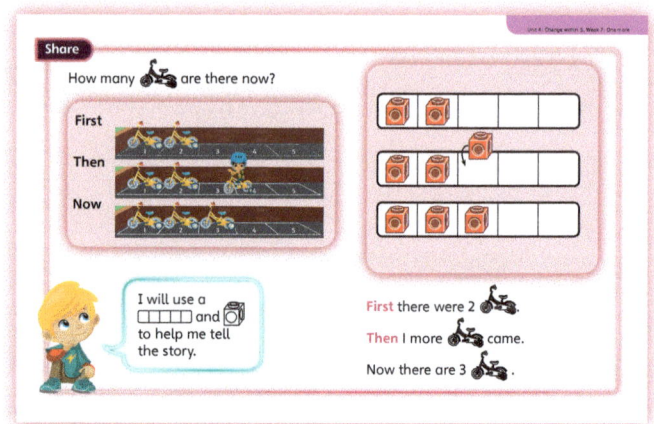

DEEPEN Give children access to different objects (teddies, plates, toy cars) and ask them to make up a first, then, now story to go with it to show that one more than 2 is 3.

GET ACTIVE Use role play to make up real-life one more stories using different resources in the classroom or outside as inspiration. Give children an example using toy animals: *First there are 4 sheep in a field, then one more sheep walks into the field, now there are 5 sheep in the field.*

Unit 4: Change within 5, Week 7: One more

Day 3

Learning focus

Exploring one more, with numbers to 5

Think together

WAYS OF WORKING Whole class or small groups
Have cubes or blocks in two different colours available for children to use to represent their first, then, now stories. Use single page mode to view the **Online Flashcard** one question at a time.

IN FOCUS This **Think together** moves children's thinking on from the familiar, concrete context in Question ❶ to thinking of one more as a mathematical concept using a five frame and cubes in Question ❷. Different numbers are used in Question ❶ and Question ❷, so that children do not build the misconception that the answer to one more is always the same.

ASK

- Question ❶: Refer to what Flo is saying to get children started. *How many bikes are there at first? What happens then? How many bikes are there now?*
- Question ❷: *What is different about this picture? How many cubes are there at first? What is the same about the story? Can you act out the story using cubes? One more than 4 is 5, let's repeat that together.*

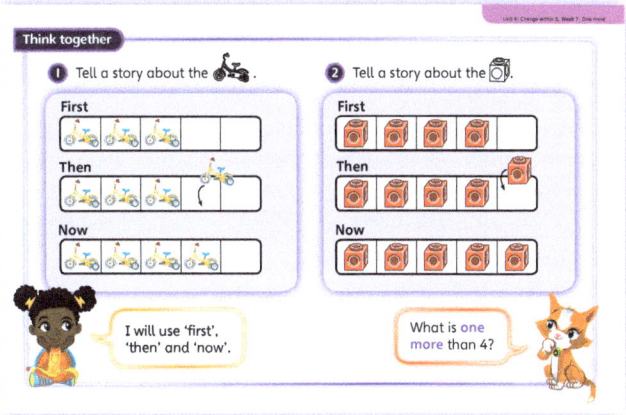

STRENGTHEN Check answers by counting together. For children who are misunderstanding, go back to a physical activity to reinforce the concept. Physically add one more to a group of 3 cars, teddies or children, for example, then support children to model the activity using the five frame and cubes.

DEEPEN Tell children a first, then, now story and ask them to recreate the story on the five frames, using cubes. In pairs they could then create their own story for their partner to show on a five frame.

Practice: Journal 1

WAYS OF WORKING Independent thinking

IN FOCUS The focus of this **Practice** activity is to reinforce the vocabulary of *one more* and the *first*, *then*, *now* sequence of adding one more, so that children feel confident when adding one more independently. For the second part, encourage children to show one more than 3 with physical objects on the page first, then record this in their **Maths Journal** by drawing their objects into the five frame.

MASTERY CHECKPOINT Children who have mastered this concept can say the number that is one more than a number below 5. At this stage, children have not explored 0, so they will not necessarily know that one more than 0 is 1.

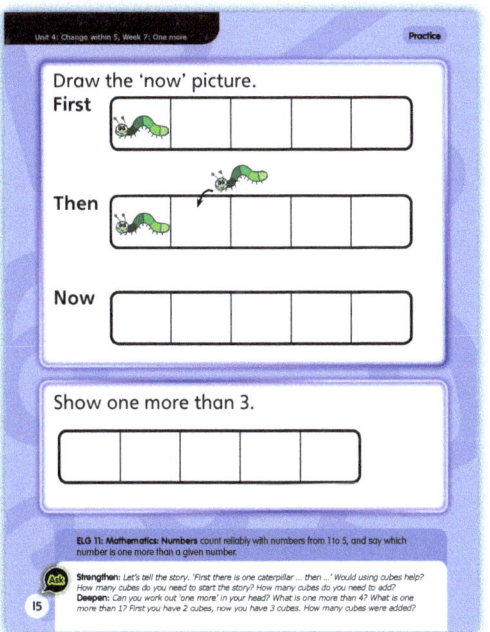

71

Unit 4: Change within 5, Week 7: One more

Day 4

Learning focus

Ordering one more stories

Challenge

WAYS OF WORKING Whole class or small groups
The whole class should attempt this **Challenge**, but with those who have not yet mastered the concept of one more working closely with adult support and using real objects and stem sentences to support them. As children may not recognise the objects as cars, draw this out in the discussion. This conversaton will help to develop their spacial awareness. Encourage children to look down at toy cars from above, and in a five frame, to strengthen this point.

IN FOCUS Children use their understanding of first, then, now to order the story. They use cars to act out the story. Encourage children to describe what they are doing and to use the language of *one more*.

ASK

- *Can you use a five frame and cars or cubes? How can you show me you have found the right order?*
- *Can you tell a first, then, now story about the cars? What happened first? Then what happened?*
- *Is Ash correct? Is this a one more story?*

STRENGTHEN Children will need adult support and access to lots of concrete manipulatives. Encourage children to count aloud as they work through the activity. Prompt children with the first, then, now story structure they have been using and, if necessary, support them by modelling the story for them. Encourage them to think of their own one more first, then, now stories.

DEEPEN To deepen understanding, ask children to work with a partner. Each child makes up their own one more story using objects from around the room. One child in each pair then tells their story to their partner who shows the story on a five frame.

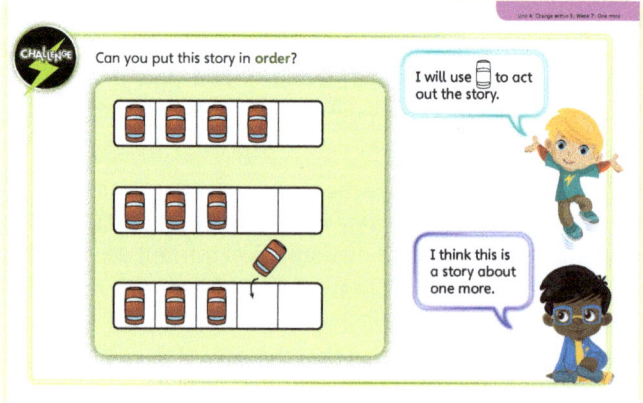

Unit 4: Change within 5, Week 7: One more

Day 5

Learning focus
Applying one more stories

Practical activities

WAYS OF WORKING Whole class or small groups

IN FOCUS These **Practical activities** strengthen and consolidate understanding of finding one more. Encourage children to explore one more stories in a variety of practical contexts. It is important that children can see and hear what one more looks like before attempting to show it in abstract forms.

GET ACTIVE **Please may I have one more?**
Show children 2, 3 or 4 of an item (teddy, plate, car, for example) and ask pairs of children, in turn, to go and get you one more of the same item. Help all children to tell the story, repeating each phrase after you if necessary.

One more on the line
Use a washing line and socks to show one more. Say: *First there are 3 socks, then one more is hung on the line, now there are 4 socks.*

Jump one more
Put children in pairs. Say a number 1–4 and ask one child in each pair to do that many jumps, counting them as they go. The second child then has to do one more jump than their partner, counting as they go. Ask children to repeat after you what has happened. Say: *3 is one more than 2*.

Clap one more
Explain to children that you are going to clap 2, 3 or even 4 times, so they need to listen carefully because they should clap back to you with one more clap than you did. After each action use the phrase *one more than (3) is (4)* to reinforce the language.

Reflect: Journal 2

WAYS OF WORKING Independent thinking

IN FOCUS The focus of this **Reflect** activity is for children to show they can represent one more than a number up to 4 in a variety of ways. Guide children using the questions at the bottom of the page. Encourage children to verbalise their first, then, now stories before attempting to draw them. The page scaffolds the structure to help them get started.

MASTERY CHECKPOINT **Children who have mastered this concept** can independently describe and show one more using manipulatives and in a drawing.

Children who have not yet mastered this concept need support and prompts to show one more.

Children who have mastered this concept with greater depth can make up a variety of stories to describe and then show one more, using a variety of contexts and/or manipulatives.

Unit 4: Change within 5, Week 8: One less

One less

Learning focus

This week, children will learn about finding one less than a given number within 5 using concrete objects and pictures to help them. They will use role play and first, then, now stories to explore one less. Crossing out, not rubbing out, should be used when representing one less pictorially.

Small steps

→ Previous step: One more
→ **This step: One less**
→ Next step: My day

COMMON MISCONCEPTIONS

Children may get confused when finding one less and think that the answer is 1 because they have taken one thing away. Children may also confuse one less with one more. Encourage children to associate *one less* with *crossing one out* so that they can clearly visualise the concept. Ask:
- What does one less mean? How can you show me one less?

KEY LANGUAGE

In lesson: one, two, three, four, five, 0, 1, 2, 3, 4, 5, none, count, **forwards**, **backwards**, first, then, now, how many, **one less**

Other language to be used by the teacher: zero, number story, fewer, take away

STRUCTURES AND REPRESENTATIONS

multilink cubes, five frames

RESOURCES

Mandatory: multilink cubes, five frames

Optional: small toys for counting, laminated print outs of numerals 1–5 (photocopiables 2–6), building blocks, pictures of towers made from blocks, items for setting a table, pictures of natural treasures, mini whiteboards, washing line, pegs, socks

EXPLORE

Taking every opportunity throughout the school day to build and reinforce mathematical concepts gives children's learning purpose and meaning in the wider context of their lives.

ACTIVITY	AREA	DESCRIPTION	RESOURCES
Set the table	Home corner	Ask children to set the table for 3 people then take a pretend phone call and explain that one less person is coming so they can take away a place.	Plates, cups and other items to lay the table
Find one less than a number	Classroom	Children take a number then find objects to show one less than their number.	Laminated print outs of numerals 1–5 (photocopiables 2–6)
Find one less than an amount	Outside	Show pictures from the natural environment with 2–5 items on each. Ask children to find one less than the number shown on the picture.	Pictures of natural treasures such as leaves, shells, pebbles, conkers
Build one less	Anywhere	Show a picture of a tower and ask children to build a tower with one less block. Repeat with different sizes of tower, up to 5 blocks high.	Pictures of towers made of blocks. Some all one colour, and some made of two or more colours.

Unit 4: Change within 5, Week 8: One less

Day 1

Learning focus
Finding one less

Before you teach
- Are all children secure with one-to-one correspondence of numbers to 5?
- Can all children count backwards from 5?
- Do children understand what the word *less* means?

Starter

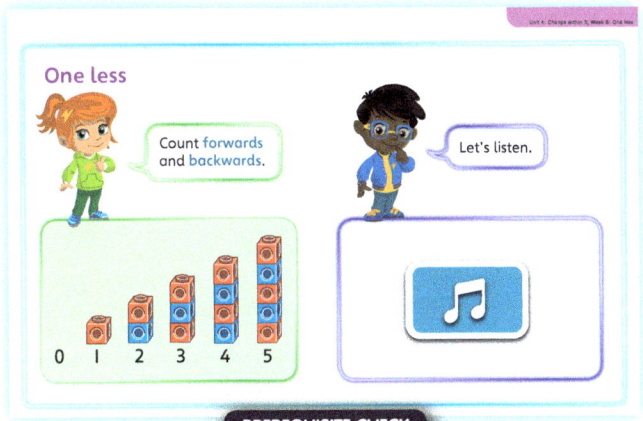

PREREQUISITE CHECK Counting forwards and backwards within 5.

WAYS OF WORKING Whole class

IN FOCUS The **Prerequisite check** ensures stable counting to and from 5. Fluency and confidence with this skill is an important starting point for this week's learning.

ASK
- *Can you count the towers?*
- *Can you count them from 0–5? Can you count them from 5–0?*

Song: 5 in the bed
There were 5 in a bed and the little one said, 'Roll over, roll over.' So they all rolled over and one fell out.
There were 4 in a bed and the little one said, 'Roll over, roll over.' So they all rolled over and one fell out.
There were 3 in a bed and the little one said, 'Roll over, roll over.' So they all rolled over and one fell out.
There were 2 in a bed and the little one said, 'Roll over, roll over.' So they all rolled over and one fell out.
There was 1 in a bed and the little one said, 'Roll over, roll over.' So they all rolled over and one fell out.
There were none in the bed.
5, 4, 3, 2, 1 … none!

STIMULUS

STIMULUS Song: 5 in the bed

IN FOCUS The song in this **Stimulus** is designed to prompt children to think about one less and will give children an image of one less. It can be referred to throughout the week to help consolidate understanding of this key concept.

ASK
- *How many children are in the bed at the start?*
- *How many children are in the bed now that one has fallen out? How many will be in bed at the end of the song?*
- *Are the numbers going up or down? How do you know?*

GET ACTIVE Arrange children into groups of 5 and encourage them to act out the song. They can pretend to lie in a bed, and roll over to symbolise one of them falling out. Prompt children to describe what is happening: *Every time one person rolls over they fall out of bed, so now there is one less person in bed.* Ask: *What will happen when the next person falls out of bed?* Guide them towards: *There will be one less person in bed.*

Unit 4: Change within 5, Week 8: One less

Day 2

Learning focus
Finding one less with number stories

Discover

WAYS OF WORKING Whole class or small groups
Have plenty of countable objects available for children to make up their own stories. Think about using both inside and outside areas to consolidate the activity.

IN FOCUS The **Discover** focuses on exploring what happens when one is taken away from a group. Children should be encouraged to use their imagination to make up first, then, now stories to show one less. Ensure that children do not use numbers beyond 5 at this stage.

ASK
- How many children are on the swings at first? Then what happens? How many children are on the swings now?
- Can you tell a first, then, now story about the birds in the picture?
- How many have been taken away each time?

STRENGTHEN If children are struggling with telling a one less story, offer them stem sentences to complete: **First** there are … children, **then** … child leaves, **now** there are … children. One less than 3 is … .

DEEPEN Ask children to think of their own one less stories to tell to a partner using the 'first, then, now' story structure. Encourage partners to share stories, including a statement at the end: One less than … is … .

Share

WAYS OF WORKING Whole class

IN FOCUS The one less story is now shown using concrete and pictorial representations. Ensure, when showing one less pictorially, children use crossing out rather than rubbing out. This helps children to see what they started with and to see what they have left.

ASK
- What does 1 cube show? What do 2 cubes show? What do 3 cubes show?
- What does the first picture show? Then what happens in the second picture? Now what does the third picture show?
- Why is this one crossed out? What is one less than 3?

STRENGTHEN Give children access to cubes to recreate the sequence in the pictures. Encourage children to say their first, then, now stories out loud and to physically move the cubes to show what is happening. Use mini whiteboards so that children can practise drawing up to 5 shapes and crossing one out.

DEEPEN Challenge children to explore one less than 1. Can they write or draw a first, then, now story about this? To

extend and deepen learning opportunities, children could draw their own comic strips to show a first, then, now story.

GET ACTIVE Children could role-play being kind to others by giving them something of theirs. Encourage correct language and use of full sentences throughout. For example: I have 3 toys, I give my friend 1 toy, now I have 2 toys. I have one less toy than I had at the beginning. One less than 3 is 2. I now have fewer toys than I started with.

76

Unit 4: Change within 5, Week 8: One less

Day 3

Learning focus

Exploring one less, with numbers to 5

Think together

WAYS OF WORKING Whole class or small groups
Have cubes available for children to use to represent their first, then, now stories.

IN FOCUS Question ❶ explores one less related to a shortened version of the song '10 green bottles': *5 green bottles, hanging on the wall* (×2) *and if one green bottle should accidentally fall, there'll be 4 green bottles hanging on the wall*. As you sing, model what is happening using cubes to represent the bottles, moving one to the side as it 'falls'. Encourage children to represent what is happening in the picture, using cubes and a five frame to help scaffold their approach. Question ❷ moves children towards a more abstract approach by using pictorial representations and models to show one less.

ASK

- Question ❶: *Do you know the song this question is showing? Let's sing it.*
- Question ❶: *Let's use cubes to represent the green bottles. How many cubes will you need to start with? How many cubes will you take away in each part of the song? How many cubes will you have left at the end of the song?*
- Question ❷: *What happens first? Then what happens? What does the crossing out show? Now what happens?*
- Question ❷: *Can you use the words 'take away' in your story? What do they mean?*

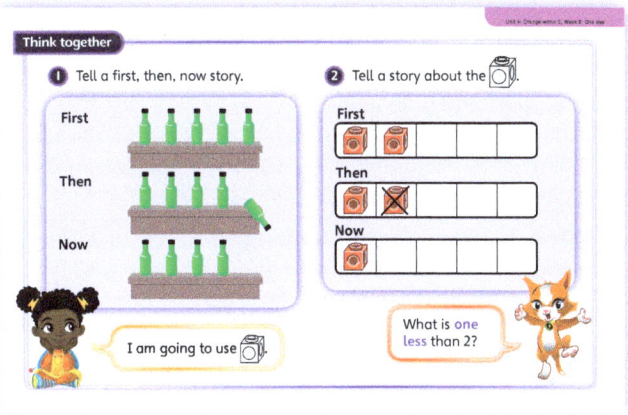

STRENGTHEN Check answers to Question ❶ and Question ❷ by counting together. Sing the song again or a different counting down song, stopping after each verse. Each child starts with 5 cubes to represent the items, moving one to the side each time. State what is happening for children to repeat: **First** we had 5 bottles, **then** one bottle fell off the wall, so **now** we have 4 bottles. One less than 5 is 4.

DEEPEN Read children some first, then, now stories about one less and ask them to recreate the stories on five frames. Vary the stories using different numbers up to 5 to help deepen understanding. Encourage children to draw pictures and use crossing out to show one less.

Practice: Journal 1

WAYS OF WORKING Independent thinking

IN FOCUS The focus of this **Practice** activity is to reinforce the vocabulary of *one less* and ensure that children understand what this means: a five frame and cubes help children to visualise this.

MASTERY CHECKPOINT Children who have mastered this concept can tell you the number that is one less than a number up to 5 and demonstrate this understanding using a variety of objects in different contexts.

77

Unit 4: Change within 5, Week 8: One less

Day 4

Learning focus

Ordering one less stories

Challenge

WAYS OF WORKING Whole class

The whole class should attempt this **Challenge**, but provide adult support and manipulatives for those who are less confident. Children could work in pairs to discuss which part is missing. Encourage children to use the language of *first*, *then*, *now* to establish that the *then* part is missing.

IN FOCUS The focus of this **Challenge** is to consolidate what children have been learning about one less and reorder the question so that they are working out what happened in the middle – the *then* part of first, then, now. Encourage children to describe to a partner what has happened in the picture. Can they tell each other a story about it?

This would be a good time to embed understanding of the concept of one less by exploring it in different areas of the classroom. Refer to **Explore** on page 74 for some activity ideas.

ASK

- *Can you tell a first, then, now story about the bees? What do you think happened to one of the bees?*
- *How can you show that you are correct?*
- *Can you use a five frame and cubes to show what happened?*
- *Can you draw the story of the bees? How will you show one less?*

STRENGTHEN For children who are not yet confident with one less, talk them through each part, using the language of *first*, *then*, *now* and manipulatives to represent the bees. Children could represent the bees with interlocking cubes, one next to the other, to show that the *now* cubes are one less than the *first* cubes. Encourage children to count out loud.

DEEPEN To deepen understanding of the concept of one less, prompt thinking by asking: *What is one less than 1? If there is just 1 sheep in a field and then that sheep runs away, how many are there now? Can you show this on a five frame? Can you make up a different story to match what you have shown me on the five frame?* Explain that the numeral to show none is 0.

Unit 4: Change within 5, Week 8: One less

Day 5

Learning focus
Applying one less stories

Practical activities

WAYS OF WORKING Small groups

IN FOCUS The aim of the **Practical activities** is to encourage confident, flexible thinking about one less, in more abstract terms. Encourage the use of verbal first, then, now stories with each activity. It is important that children see what one less looks like in a variety of contexts. Allow children to use cubes to replicate the task if necessary.

GET ACTIVE **Musical chairs**
Work with 5 children at a time. Place 5 chairs out and play some music for them to dance around to. When you stop the music they all sit on a chair. After each round remove a chair so that fewer children can sit on a chair. The last child sitting wins the game! Ensure between each round you get children to describe what has happened. Say: *First there were 5 chairs, then 1 was taken away, now there are 4 chairs.*

One less on the line
Use a washing line and socks to show one less. *There are 3 socks hanging on the washing line. Take 1 sock off. First there were 3 socks, then 1 was taken away, now there are 2 socks. One less than 3 is 2*. Repeat with different starting numbers up to 5. Consider starting with one sock, too. Make the link with one more if appropriate: *2 is one less than 3, 3 is one more than 2.*

Reflect: Journal 2

WAYS OF WORKING Independent thinking

IN FOCUS The focus of this **Reflect** activity is for children to show independently that they can represent one less than a number up to 5 using pictures and crossing out one. Suggest starting with 5 if children are unsure how to begin. Use the prompt questions at the bottom of the page to support children as necessary and encourage them to share their stories with a partner.

MASTERY CHECKPOINT **Children who have mastered this concept** can show independently one less than 5 using a variety of objects or drawings.

Children who have not yet mastered this concept need support and prompts to complete their one less story.

Children who have mastered this concept with greater depth can say that 4 is one less than 5 and make up a first, then, now story describing one less than 5. Children will also be comfortable and confident with one less than 1.

Unit 5
Time

Mastery Expert tip! "Display the daily routines of the class using visual representations of children arriving at school, doing Maths, having snacks, lunchtime, story time and getting ready for home time. Use the language of time throughout the day, drawing children's attention to the classroom clock: *It's 3 o'clock. Let's tidy up!*"

Don't forget watch the Working with measure video

ELGs

This unit supports the following ELGs:

→ **ELG 12: Mathematics: Shape, space and measures**
use everyday language to talk about size, weight, capacity, position, distance, time and money to compare quantities and objects and to solve problems
recognise, create and describe patterns

→ **ELG 3: Communication and language: Speaking**
develop their own narratives and explanations by connecting ideas or events

→ **ELG 13: Understanding the world: People and communities**
talk about past and present events in their own lives and in the lives of family members
know about similarities and differences between themselves and others, and among families, communities and traditions

WHY THIS UNIT IS IMPORTANT

This unit focuses on drawing children's attention to the sequencing of activities and events in their day. The unit helps children develop a sense of time in terms of daily routine that will give them the foundation skills they will need for further work on time in Year 1. There are clear literacy links within the unit as it begins with understanding and discussing the story in the **Starter** and then focuses on encouraging children to develop their own narratives and explanations by connecting ideas or events.

WAYS OF WORKING

Use the language of time throughout the day: *First we are going to … then we will … after that it will be lunchtime.* Ensure children have access to clocks that can be referred to at key points in the day so that they become familiar with them.

WHERE THIS UNIT FITS

→ Unit 4: Change within 5
→ **Unit 5: Time**
→ Year 1, Unit 17: Time

This unit stands alone in Reception, although the first, then, now stories used in Unit 4 will have provided a helpful foundation for sequencing, and will lay the foundations for work on time in Key Stage 1.

Link to Key Stage 1

Measurement
- sequence events in chronological order using language [for example, before and after, next, first, today, yesterday, tomorrow, morning, afternoon and evening]

This unit continues to develop children's sense of chronology using familiar events in their day.

Unit 5: Time

ASSESSING MASTERY

Children who have mastered this unit will be able to:
- order three familiar events from their day
- discuss what is happening in each picture
- use the language related to time: before, after, next, then, later

COMMON MISCONCEPTIONS	STRENGTHENING UNDERSTANDING	GOING DEEPER
Children may not understand the vocabulary related to time.	Build the vocabulary into everyday routines to embed the language into real situations, for example: *First we wash our hands, then we … after lunch we will …*	Give examples of the vocabulary when introducing it to children, putting it into context in a sentence. **Before** *I go to bed, I clean my teeth.*
Children may not grasp the abstract nature of time and find it difficult to remember, for example, if they have had lunch.	Use sequencing activities to strengthen understanding: retelling familiar stories in sequence, un-muddling visual timetables, making picture sequences for cooking instructions.	Encourage children to draw pictures of familiar events in their day and order them. Point out the position of the hour hand on the clock at intervals throughout the day.
Children may not have a regular routine at home and struggle with the context of *after school*.	Talk about events that are consistent for all the class, such as the routine at school. The context is less important than developing a secure sense of sequence.	When children are reading books, including wordless ones, develop their sense of sequencing by pausing and asking: *What happened first? What happened next?*

STRUCTURES AND REPRESENTATIONS

Clock faces: Although clocks do not feature on the **Online Flashcards** or in the **Maths Journal**, teachers should draw children's attention to the classroom clock at key times of day to familiarise children with clocks.

RESOURCES

Mandatory: pictures or photographs of different times of the day, variety of clock faces

Optional: camera, teaching clock, stories that include times of the day and about nocturnal animals, sand timer or stopwatch, times of the day props: toothbrush, towel, plate, cereal boxes, coat, school bag, laminated photos of children at various times of day, laminated labels and related clock faces, flute (or picture of a flute), playdough or baking equipment and a simple recipe, photocopiable 9

TEACHING TOOLS

clock

KEY LANGUAGE

There is some key language that children will need to know as part of the learning in this unit:

→ **first**, **next**, **later**, then
→ **before**, **after**, every day
→ time, clock face, o'clock
→ order, timetable, sequence

Unit 5: Time, Week 9: My day

My day

Learning focus

This week, children will be introduced to the concept of times of the day and the order of events in a day. They will begin to order familiar events using clues from pictures and will be introduced to the idea that the clock tells the time of the day, without having to read the clock.

Small steps

→ Previous step: One less
→ **This step: My day**
→ Next step: Introducing the part-whole model

COMMON MISCONCEPTIONS

Children may be unfamiliar with the order of events that build to make a day or find it difficult to keep track of events. Take every opportunity to draw children's attention to the language of time and to the clock face at key times during the day. Ask:
- *Do you put your coat on your peg before or after you come into class? What did you have for lunch?*
- *It is nearly home time because the clock says almost 3 o'clock – what do you need to do to get ready?*

KEY LANGUAGE

In lesson: first, next, later, then, before, after

Other language to be used by the teacher: time, clock face, o'clock, order, timetable, sequence

STRUCTURES AND REPRESENTATIONS

clock faces

RESOURCES

Mandatory: clock faces, pictures to represent key times of the day, photocopiable 9

Optional: camera, teaching clock, books that include stories about times of the day and/or stories of nocturnal animals, sand timer or stopwatch, times of the day props, laminated photos of children at various times of day, laminated labels and related clock faces, flute (or picture of a flute), playdough or baking equipment and a simple recipe

EXPLORE

Taking every opportunity throughout the school day to build and reinforce mathematical concepts gives children's learning purpose and meaning in the wider context of their lives. To embed and reinforce understanding of the concept of time, build the activities below into your everyday class routine, not only during this unit, but throughout the year.

ACTIVITY	AREA	DESCRIPTION	RESOURCES
Clock faces	Classroom or hall	Draw attention to clocks at different times of the day, for example: *Look, it's 12 o'clock, it is time for lunch.*	Analogue clocks around school
Visual timetable display board	Classroom	Make a display board of o'clock times relating to the school day, including clock faces showing the times. Ask children to match the photos to the correct time of day by discussing and sequencing the day's events.	Laminated photos of children at different times of the day, for example, registration, playtime, lunchtime, home time. Laminated labels and related clock faces
Nocturnal animals	Classroom	Read books and create pictures of nocturnal animals. Use these as a prompt for discussion about day and night and the difference between them.	Books and pictures of nocturnal animals

Unit 5: Time, Week 9: My day

Day 1

Learning focus

Why do we need to tell the time?

Starter

Before you teach

- What prompts will you provide to spark discussion about why we need to tell the time?
- What resources will you provide to help familiarise children with ordering events in a day?
- How will you support children's understanding of how times of the day form the basis of a daily routine or timetable?

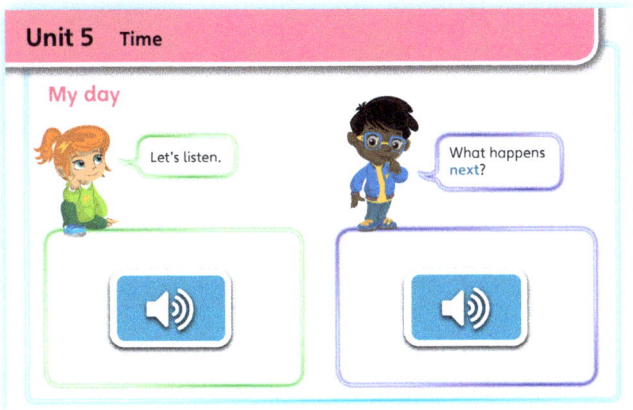

STIMULUS Story: Running late (part 1)

Elsa was always late. She was late getting out of bed. She was late down to the kitchen for breakfast. Sometimes she was even late getting to school. On Monday morning, Elsa was excited. She was going to have her first flute lesson at school!

She jumped out of bed and ran downstairs for breakfast. Then she packed her flute in its special case and took it to school with her. She waited impatiently all through the register. 'I'm having a flute lesson today!' She told her teacher, proudly. 'It's at ten o'clock.'

'That's wonderful!' said her teacher. 'But first we have maths.' Elsa and her friends sat on the carpet, and the teacher began their maths lesson.

'Today, we're learning to tell the time,' said the teacher. Elsa tried very hard during maths. She looked at the clock on the wall, but she didn't know how to tell the time yet.

Next, it was phonics. 'D-r-u-m,' sounded out Elsa. 'Drum!' Elsa gasped.

'Oh no! I'm late for my flute lesson!' Elsa picked up her flute and hurried down the corridor to her flute lesson.

'You're late!' said the music teacher. 'Now you've missed your lesson! We don't have time today.'

'Oh no!' said Elsa.

WAYS OF WORKING Whole class

IN FOCUS The story prompts important discussion about why it is important to tell the time – the focus for the learning in this unit.

ASK

- How do you think Elsa was feeling?
- What can Elsa do next week to help her?

STIMULUS 2 Story: Running late (part 2)

At home time, Elsa was still upset. 'What's wrong?' asked Dad at the school gate.

'I missed my flute lesson,' moaned Elsa. 'I was too late!'

'Don't worry,' said Dad. 'I think I have an idea to make sure you don't miss it next time.' At home, Elsa sat at the kitchen table while Dad fetched some paper and colouring pencils for her.

First, Elsa drew a picture of herself arriving at school. Then, she drew a picture of herself in a maths lesson. Next, she drew a picture of herself playing the flute. She looked at her drawings.

'First, I go to school,' said Elsa. 'Then, I do maths. Next, I go to my flute lesson.'

'I'll never miss my flute lesson again!' said Elsa, happily.

IN FOCUS Show children a flute or a picture of a flute as an additional stimulus. The second part of the story introduces the concept of the order of events in the day. Introduce children to the language of *first*, *next*, *then* and *later*.

ASK

- *What has Elsa done to help her not miss another lesson? How will this help her? What do you do to make sure you do not miss important things?*
- *How many sleeps until Elsa's next flute lesson? So how many days is that?*

GET ACTIVE Place a variety of types of clocks that show different o'clock times around the room and encourage children to explore them. Ask: *Do you recognise any of the numbers? Can you see any patterns? Why do you think you need to learn to tell the time?* Children are not expected to tell the time using the clock face at this point.

Unit 5: Time, Week 9: My day

Day 2

Learning focus
Ordering familiar events in a typical day

Discover

WAYS OF WORKING Whole class or small groups
Provide copies of photocopiable 9 (page 101) showing the pictures in **Discover** for children to put in order.

IN FOCUS The **Discover** picture shows Alex eating lunch with his friends, getting home from school, and arriving at school. By looking at what is wrong, children will begin to discuss the sequence of familiar events.

ASK
- What is happening in each picture? How do you know?
- What has happened to the order of these pictures? Why do you think that?

STRENGTHEN If children need support in sequencing familiar events, it may be useful to ask what they do first in their day. Encourage children to talk to their partner about what they do each day. Ask: *What next? How is your day the same as your partner's day? How is your day different from their day?*

DEEPEN Ask children about their own daily routines and to draw simple pictures to show getting up in the morning, being at school and going to bed. Encourage them to order their pictures.

Share

WAYS OF WORKING Whole class

IN FOCUS The focus of this **Share** is to discuss daily routines. Draw attention to Dexter's question to help guide children through daily events in order.

ASK
- What do you do first in your day? Is it the same every day?
- What is the last thing you do each day? [Some children might distinguish between school days and weekends.]

STRENGTHEN Strengthen understanding of daily routines by looking at other activities children take part in during their day. Read familiar stories, such as *Goldilocks and the Three Bears*, and encourage discussion around the sequence of events in this story using the language of *first*, *next* and *then*. Construct a visual timetable of the school day using pictures or photographs and refer to it throughout the day.

DEEPEN For children who can order three familiar events, challenge them to think about what happens in their day that would fit in between, for instance, snack time and lunchtime, or prompt them with questions such as: *We have lunch, what happens **next**? And then what do you do?*

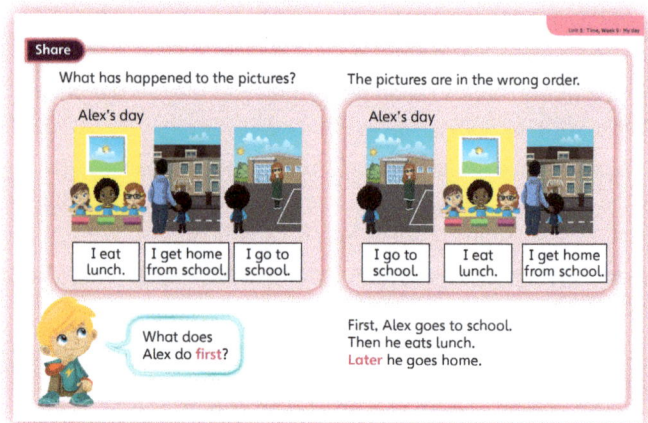

GET ACTIVE Using props, ask children to role play the sequence of their day in order using the key vocabulary *first, then, next* and *later*.

Day 3

Learning focus

Begin to describe familiar events in order, using the language of time

Think together

WAYS OF WORKING Whole class

IN FOCUS The picture shows what Alex does after school. Question ❶ practises putting familiar events in order using a new context. In Question ❷, children should begin to use the language *first, then, next, later* to tell a story of familiar activities. The pictures can be used to prompt discussion about times of the day and the order of familiar events in a day.

ASK

- Question ❶: *Put these pictures in order. What comes first? How does the sun help you to order these pictures?*
- Question ❷: *Can you describe what is happening in Alex's day? Use the language related to time!*

STRENGTHEN Support children's understanding by offering them question prompts to help them discuss what happens in their day after school. Ask: *What happens first? What time of day is light, what time of day is dark? Which comes first? What do you do when it's dark outside? What do you do when it's light outside?*

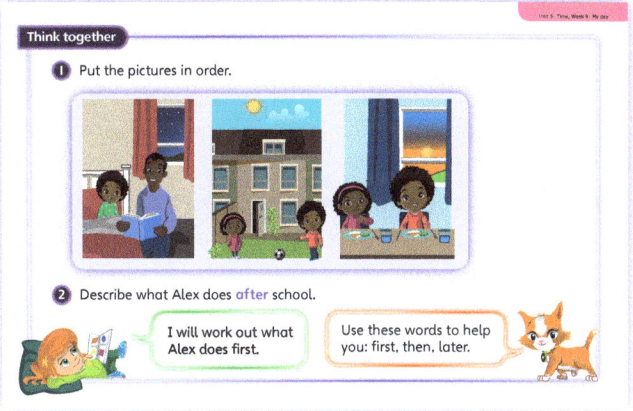

DEEPEN Encourage children to think about what happens after school in their day. Can they add to these events and order more familiar events? Do events always happen in the same order? Do they do the same things every day or are some days different?

Practice: Journal 1

WAYS OF WORKING Independent thinking

IN FOCUS This **Practice** activity allows children to practise the skill of ordering some events in a familiar day. Children use clues from the picture as a scaffold, and may be able to discuss, describe and apply observations from the previous sessions in this unit to this new context, such as the position of the sun.

MASTERY CHECKPOINT Children can confidently order these familiar events using clues from the pictures to help them, and discuss and explain how they know what is happening in the pictures using the language of time.

Unit 5: Time, Week 9: My day

Day 4

Learning focus

Begin to use the language *before* and *after*, and be able to look at the order of events flexibly, from last to first, as well as from first to last

Challenge

WAYS OF WORKING Whole class then pairs
Start by discussing the question as a whole class, and then ask children to discuss this in pairs. Ask them to feedback to the teacher in their pairs.

IN FOCUS This **Challenge** focuses on using the language of *before* to encourage children to think more flexibly about the order of familiar events in a day. For example, when describing events, we do not always describe them chronologically through a day and may describe what happened *before* an event. The focus here is on discussion and using the language of *before* and *after*, and specific stem sentences to reinforce understanding. Example sentences might include: *I have a bath before I go to bed,* or *I listen to a story after my bath.* All answers are equally valid.

ASK

- What is happening in the picture?
- What do you do before you go to bed?
- What does Alex do before he goes to bed?

STRENGTHEN Make props available to children who need support with what happens before and after, to prompt and encourage discussion. Props could include a toothbrush, hairbrush, soap and towel, box of cereal, bowl and spoon, a story book. Ask children to put the props in order as a visual representation of sequence, and encourage discussion about order using the key language of time.

DEEPEN Children can discuss and offer reasons for why some events happen in a particular order. To stimulate discussion, prompt deeper thinking by asking: *Do you clean your teeth before or after eating breakfast? Why? Do you have a story before or after your bath? Do you have a story before or after you get into bed?*

Day 5

Learning focus
Use the language of time and realise the importance of sequence

Practical activities

WAYS OF WORKING Small groups

IN FOCUS The focus of this activity is to bring to life the importance of sequence and to spark further discussion using the key vocabulary of *then, next, later, before* and *after*.

GET ACTIVE **Follow a recipe**
Provide children with the opportunity to put their new language into context by doing some baking, either real baking of a simple recipe in the kitchen or no-bake cake or playdough in the home corner of the classroom. As a group, discuss how to make cakes, including where to get ingredients from, why to follow a recipe in order and what might go wrong if you do not follow the recipe in order. Use every opportunity during this activity to model the language of *then, next, later, before* and *after*.

Reflect: Journal 2

WAYS OF WORKING Independent thinking

IN FOCUS The focus of this **Reflect** activity is to choose a way of recording events of a typical day in order. Children choose to draw three events from a typical day in sequence and should be encouraged to discuss these with a partner. This activity will also strengthen children's ability to talk about time and enable them to apply what they've learnt to their own daily routines.

MASTERY CHECKPOINT **Children who have mastered this concept** can order three familiar events from their day and discuss what is happening in each picture using the language related to time.

Children who have not yet mastered this concept can talk about familiar events in their day, some in sequence.

Children who have mastered this concept with greater depth can order three or more familiar events from their day, saying what happened before and after each event. They will be able to discuss the content of the pictures using the language related to time.

Power Maths Reception Observation Sheet

Unit 1 – Numbers to 5

Date:

Adult observing:

Children observed

Unit objective(s)
Counting to 5, forwards and backwards
- Stable order of counting to 5
- One-to-one correspondence to 5
- Cardinality to 5
- Representations to 5
- Counting to 5 and back from 5 using abstraction

What did you observe?

Try to include details such as: What prompted the behaviour? What did the children do? What did they say to you or to others? How did you (or others) respond?

Was this activity:
- [ ] Independent
- [ ] Guided
- [ ] Directed

What is the current level of mastery of the unit objective (see above)?

- [ ] **Not yet achieved mastery** – the child has not yet been able to apply the new concept without heavy guidance
- [ ] **Mastery secure** – the child can confidently and independently apply the new concept in a variety of situations
- [ ] **Mastery emerging** – the child can apply the new concept only in familiar or taught contexts or with guidance
- [ ] **Mastery with greater depth** – the child can confidently apply the new concept in a variety of situations and can manipulate the concept to investigate how it might work in new contexts

What are your next steps to help these children deepen their understanding of the concept?

© Pearson Education Ltd 2019. This page may be photocopied for use within the purchasing organisation.

Power Maths Reception Observation Sheet

Unit 2 – Sorting

Date:
Adult observing:
Children observed

Unit objective(s)
Sorting into two groups
- Explore characteristics of everyday objects
- Sorting objects where there are two distinct groups
- Discovering that objects can be sorted in different ways
- Sorting objects in more than one way
- Sorting collections of objects

What did you observe?

Try to include details such as: What prompted the behaviour? What did the children do? What did they say to you or to others? How did you (or others) respond?

Was this activity:
- [ ] Independent
- [ ] Guided
- [ ] Directed

What is the current level of mastery of the unit objective (see above)?

- [ ] **Not yet achieved mastery** – the child has not yet been able to apply the new concept without heavy guidance
- [ ] **Mastery secure** – the child can confidently and independently apply the new concept in a variety of situations
- [ ] **Mastery emerging** – the child can apply the new concept only in familiar or taught contexts or with guidance
- [ ] **Mastery with greater depth** – the child can confidently apply the new concept in a variety of situations and can manipulate the concept to investigate how it might work in new contexts

What are your next steps to help these children deepen their understanding of the concept?

© Pearson Education Ltd 2019. This page may be photocopied for use within the purchasing organisation.

Power Maths Reception Observation Sheet

Unit 3 – Comparing groups within 5

Date:

Adult observing:

Children observed

Unit objective(s)
Comparing quantities of objects within 5
- Noticing inequality of groups
- Comparing groups of identical and non-identical objects
- Using one-to-one correspondence to compare groups
- Comparing groups using more and fewer
- Realising that quantities can be equal
- Comparing groups by matching or subitising
- Representing groups to compare using cubes

What did you observe?

Try to include details such as: What prompted the behaviour? What did the children do? What did they say to you or to others? How did you (or others) respond?

Was this activity:
☐ Independent
☐ Guided
☐ Directed

What is the current level of mastery of the unit objective (see above)?

☐ **Not yet achieved mastery** – the child has not yet been able to apply the new concept without heavy guidance

☐ **Mastery secure** – the child can confidently and independently apply the new concept in a variety of situations

☐ **Mastery emerging** – the child can apply the new concept only in familiar or taught contexts or with guidance

☐ **Mastery with greater depth** – the child can confidently apply the new concept in a variety of situations and can manipulate the concept to investigate how it might work in new contexts

What are your next steps to help these children deepen their understanding of the concept?

© Pearson Education Ltd 2019. This page may be photocopied for use within the purchasing organisation.

Power Maths Reception Observation Sheet

Unit 4 – Change within 5

Date:

Adult observing:

Children observed

Unit objective(s)
Finding one more and more less
- Adding one more
- Finding one less
- Finding one more and one less with number stories
- Exploring one more and one less, with numbers to 5
- Ordering one more and one less stories
- Applying one more and one less stories

What did you observe?

Try to include details such as: What prompted the behaviour? What did the children do? What did they say to you or to others? How did you (or others) respond?

Was this activity:
☐ Independent
☐ Guided
☐ Directed

What is the current level of mastery of the unit objective (see above)?

☐ **Not yet achieved mastery** – the child has not yet been able to apply the new concept without heavy guidance

☐ **Mastery secure** – the child can confidently and independently apply the new concept in a variety of situations

☐ **Mastery emerging** – the child can apply the new concept only in familiar or taught contexts or with guidance

☐ **Mastery with greater depth** – the child can confidently apply the new concept in a variety of situations and can manipulate the concept to investigate how it might work in new contexts

What are your next steps to help these children deepen their understanding of the concept?

© Pearson Education Ltd 2019. This page may be photocopied for use within the purchasing organisation.

Power Maths Reception Observation Sheet

Unit 5 – Time

Date:

Adult observing:

Children observed

Unit objective(s)
Sequencing and using the language of time
- Understanding the purpose of being able to tell the time
- Ordering familiar events
- Begin to describe familiar events in order, using the language of time
- Look at events flexibily, from first to last as well as last to first
- Use the language of time and realise the importance of sequence

What did you observe?

Try to include details such as: What prompted the behaviour? What did the children do? What did they say to you or to others? How did you (or others) respond?

Was this activity:
☐ Independent
☐ Guided
☐ Directed

What is the current level of mastery of the unit objective (see above)?

☐ **Not yet achieved mastery** – the child has not yet been able to apply the new concept without heavy guidance

☐ **Mastery secure** – the child can confidently and independently apply the new concept in a variety of situations

☐ **Mastery emerging** – the child can apply the new concept only in familiar or taught contexts or with guidance

☐ **Mastery with greater depth** – the child can confidently apply the new concept in a variety of situations and can manipulate the concept to investigate how it might work in new contexts

What are your next steps to help these children deepen their understanding of the concept?

© Pearson Education Ltd 2019. This page may be photocopied for use within the purchasing organisation.

Photocopiable 1: Number 0

93

Photocopiable 2: Number 1

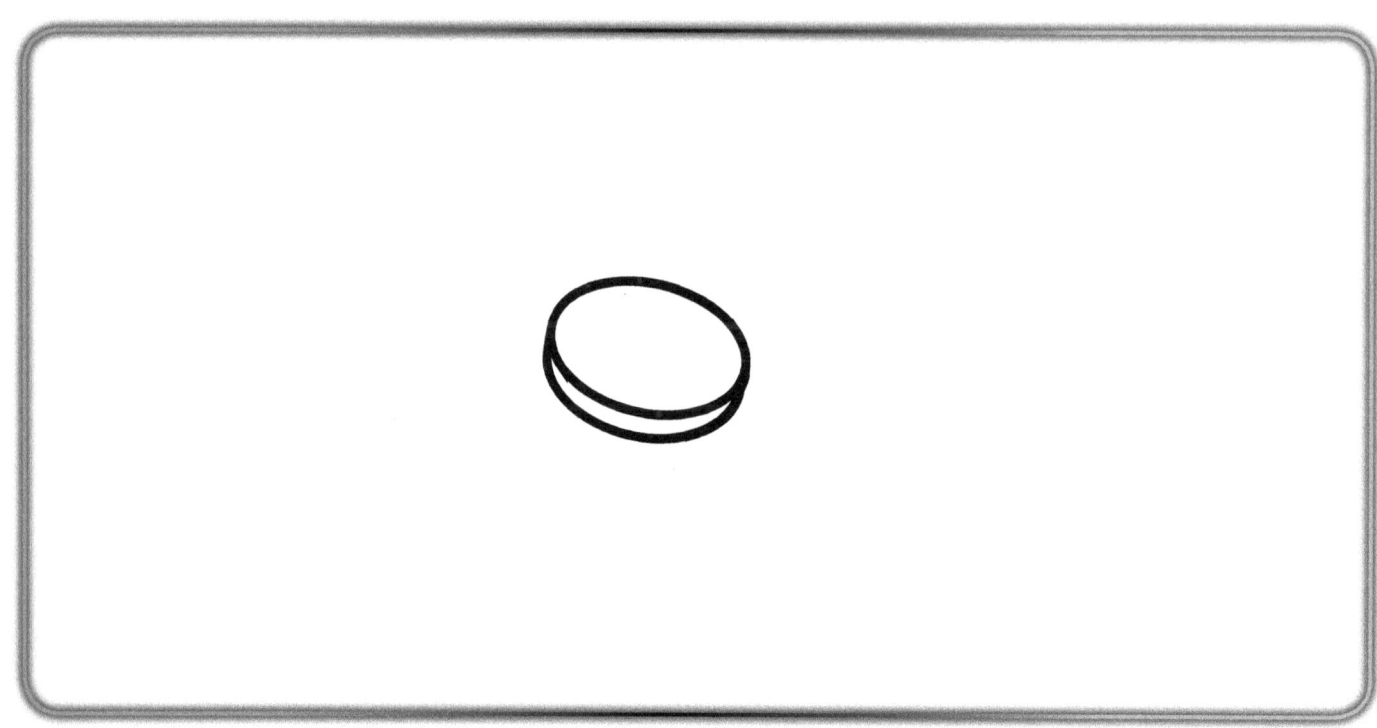

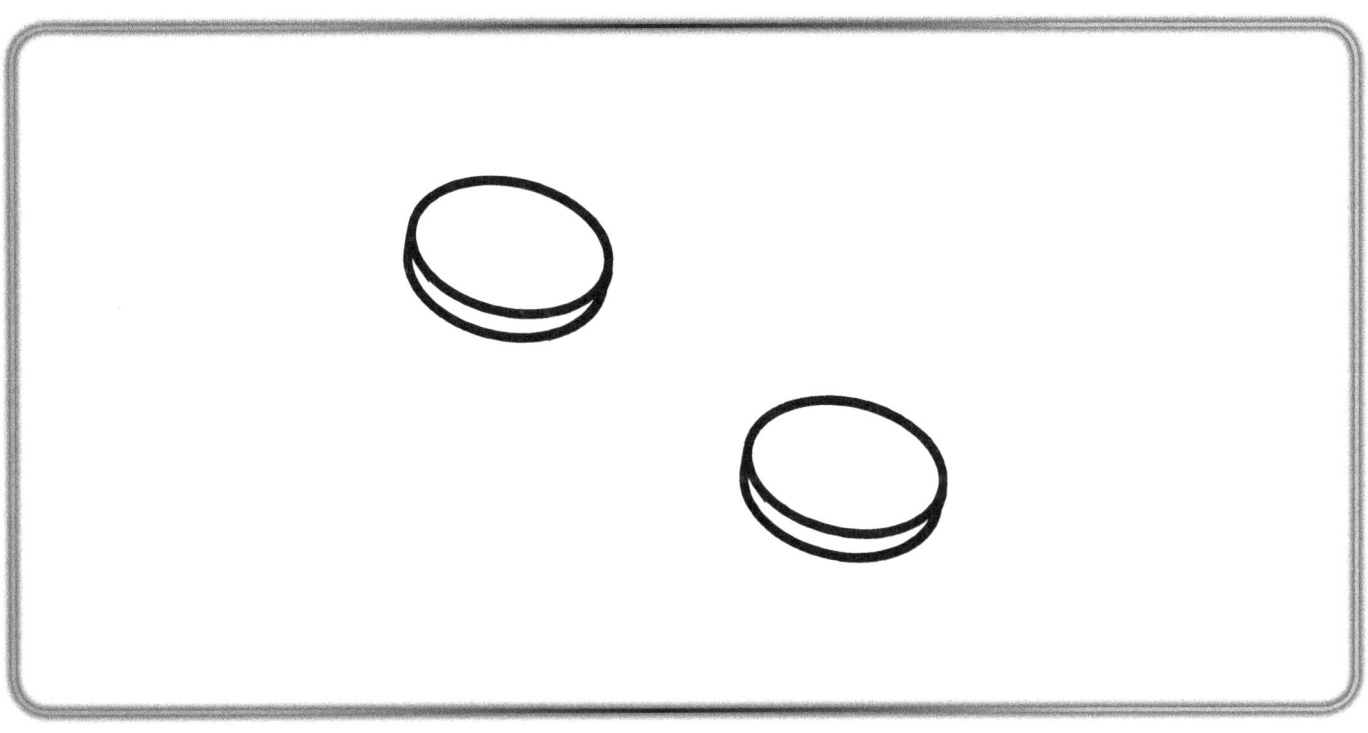

Photocopiable 4: Number 3

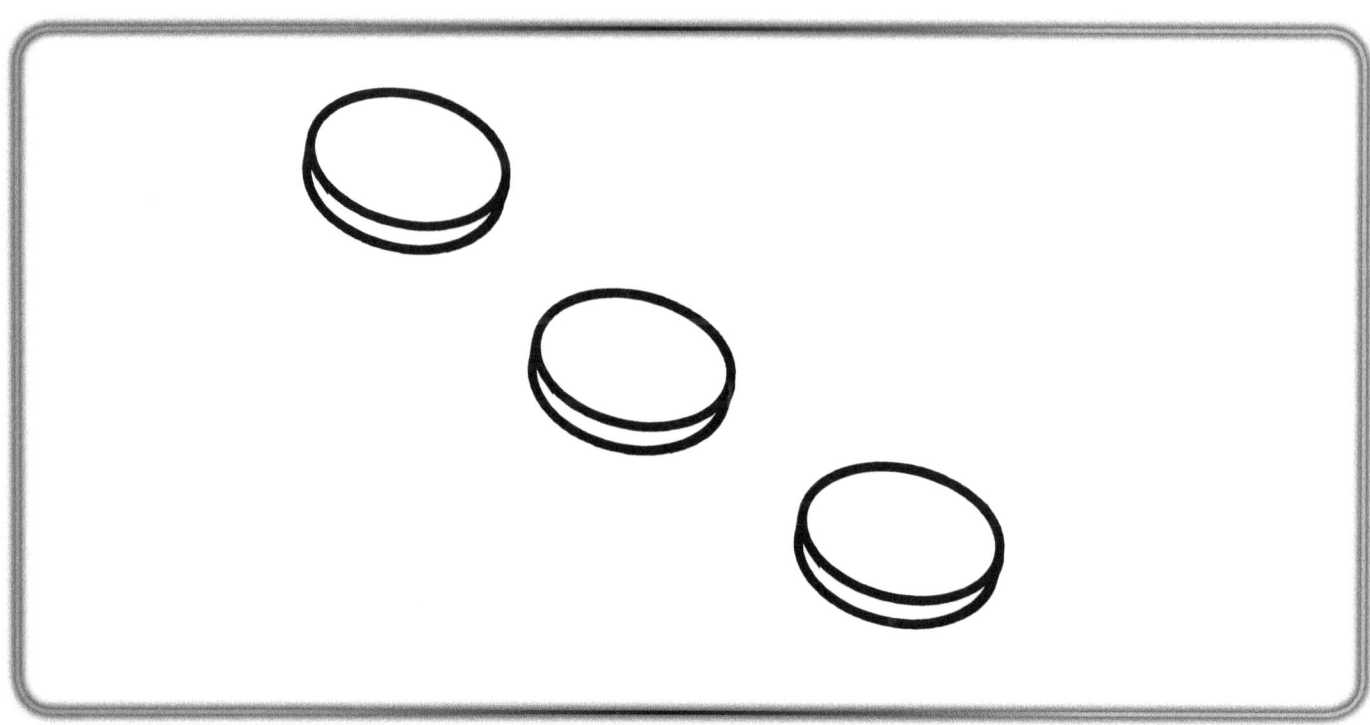

Photocopiable 5: Number 4

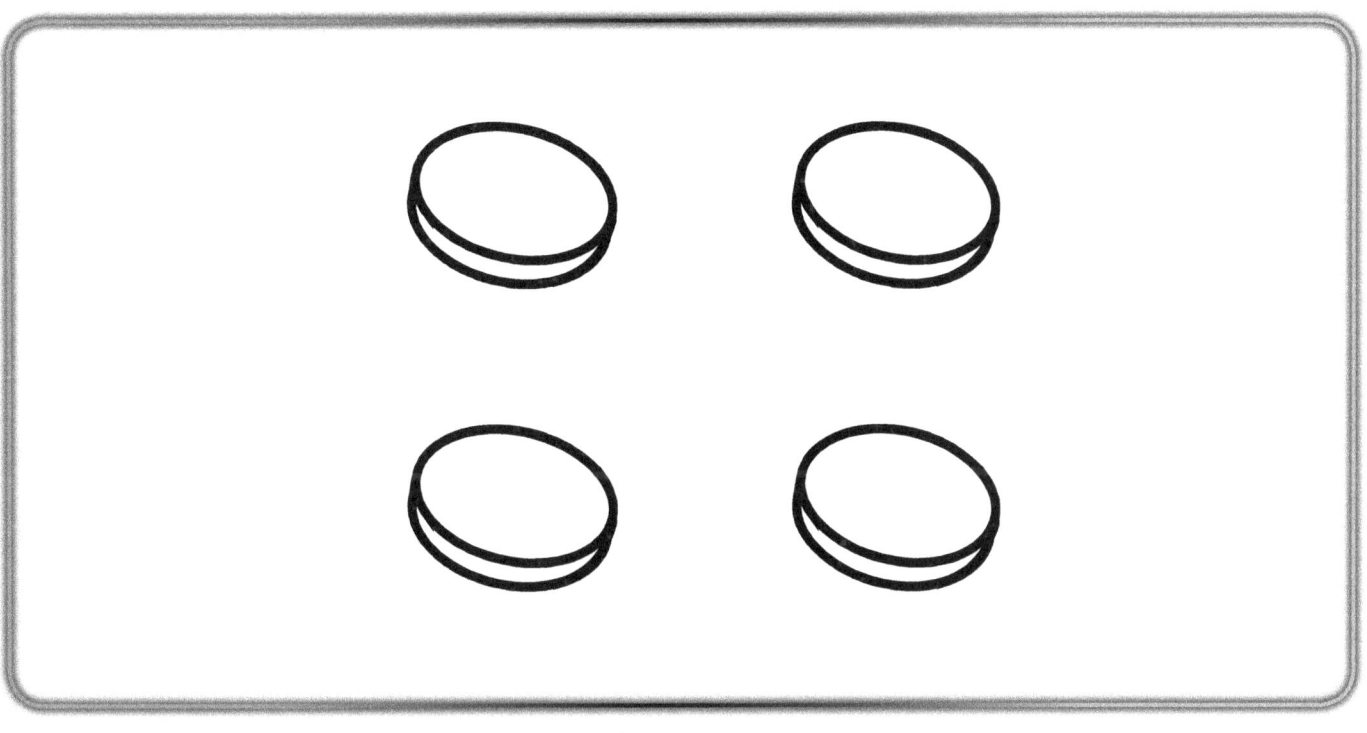

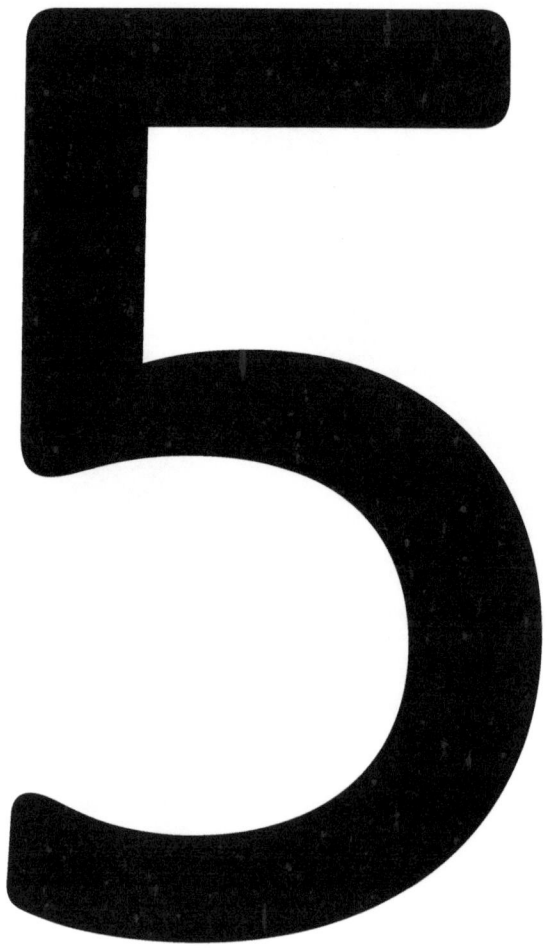
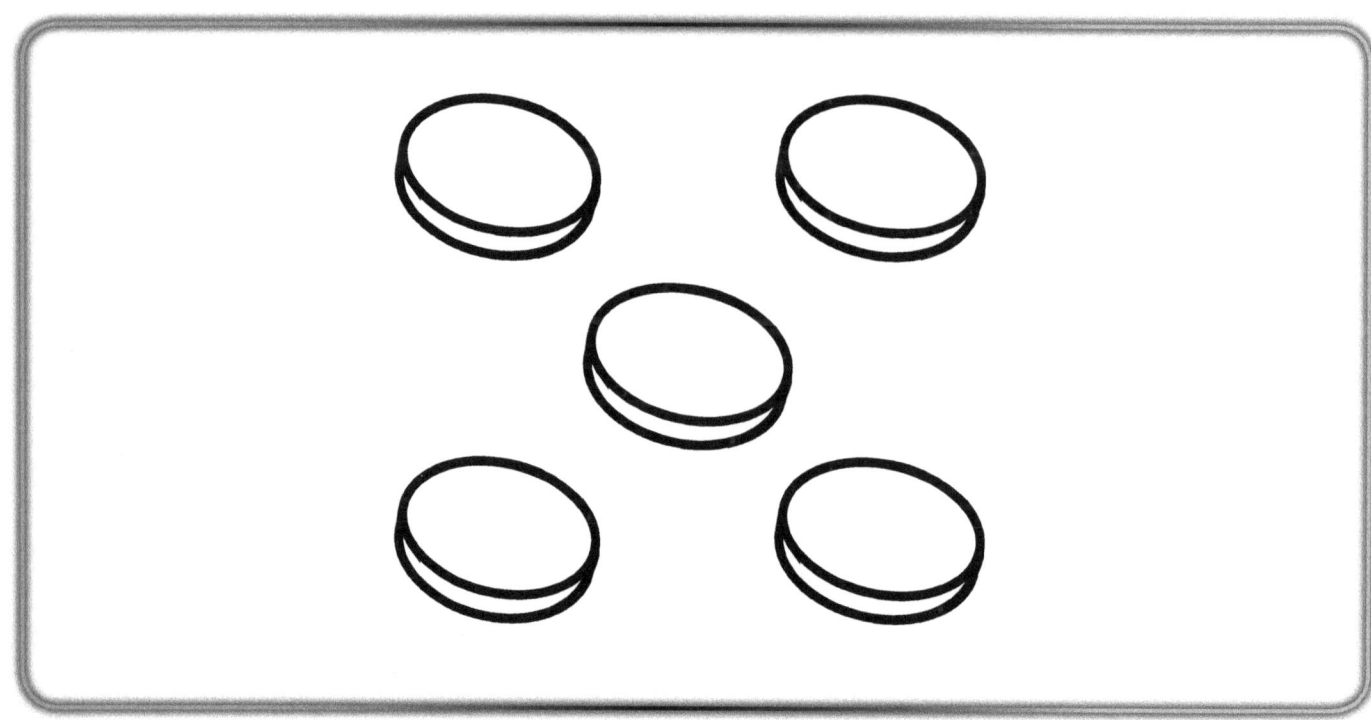

Photocopiable 7: Five frame

Photocopiable 8: Numbers to 5

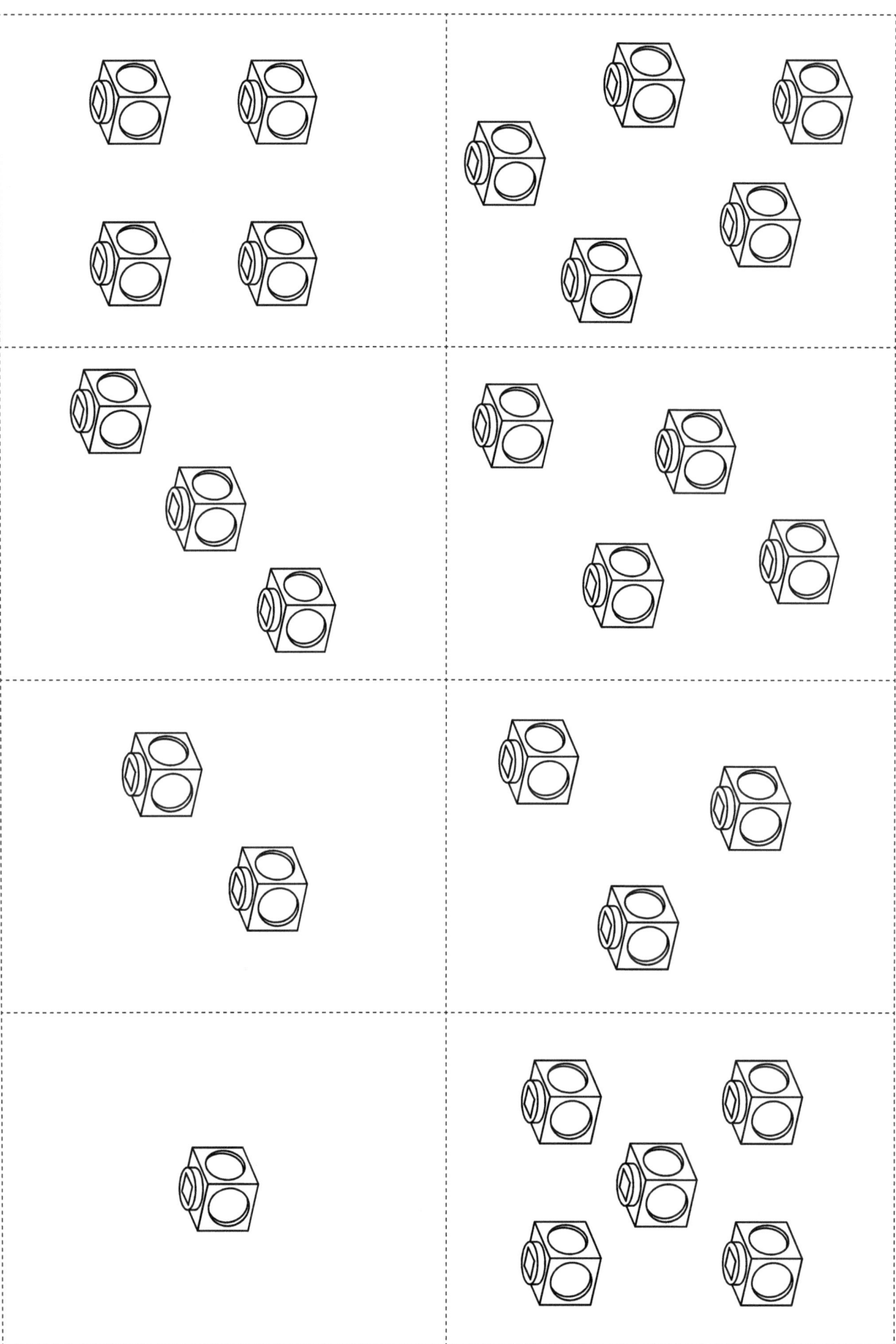

List of practical resources

Reception Term A Mandatory resources

Resource	Lesson
Analogue clock faces	**Unit 5** week 9
Buckets	**Unit 1** week 1
Candles	**Unit 1** week 3
Counters (in 2 different colours)	**Unit 2** week 4
Crayons or coloured pencils in 2 colours	**Unit 2** week 4
Five frames	**Unit 1** weeks 2, 3 **Unit 4** weeks 7, 8
Glue spatulas	**Unit 2** week 4
Multilink cubes	**Unit 1** weeks 2, 3 **Unit 3** weeks 5, 6 **Unit 4** weeks 7, 8
Numerals 1–5 (photocopiables 2–6)	**Unit 1** weeks 1, 2, 3
Pictures or photographs of times of day	**Unit 5** week 9
Paintbrushes	**Unit 2** week 4
Selection of classroom objects and real-life objects for counting and sorting, e.g. small toys, glue spatulas, bean bags, balls, leaves, conkers	**Unit 1** weeks 1, 2 **Unit 3** week 5 **Unit 4** weeks 7, 8
Sequencing pictures (photocopiable 9)	**Unit 5** week 9
Six-sided dice	**Unit 1** week 3
Spades	**Unit 1** week 1
Toy vehicles	**Unit 2** week 4

Reception Term A Optional resources

Resource	Lesson
2D shapes	**Unit 2** week 4
Bags	**Unit 3** week 5
Baskets or pots for sorting into	**Unit 2** week 4
Bean bags	**Unit 1** week 3
Bikes and parking spaces	**Unit 3** week 5
Birthday cards	**Unit 1** week 3
Buckets	**Unit 3** week 5
Building blocks	**Unit 4** weeks 7, 8
Camera	**Unit 1** week 1 **Unit 5** week 9
Chalk	**Unit 1** week 3
Containers for sorting into	**Unit 2** week 4
Digit cards	**Unit 1** week 3
Five frame	**Unit 3** week 6
Flute (or picture of a flute)	**Unit 5** week 9
Fruit and fruit bowls	**Unit 1** week 3 **Unit 3** weeks 5, 6
Glue spatulas	**Unit 2** week 4
Home corner items, including plastic plates, cups, bowls, cutlery, napkins	**Unit 1** week 3 **Unit 3** week 6 **Unit 4** weeks 7, 8

Resource	Lesson
Hoops	**Unit 1** week 3
Labels	**Unit 5** week 9
Mini whiteboards and pens	**Unit 4** week 8
Items for sequencing: cereal boxes, coat, school bag, toothbrushes, toothpaste, towel	**Unit 5** week 9
Number tracks	**Unit 3** week 5
Numerals 1–5 (photocopiables 2-6)	**Unit 4** weeks 7, 8
Opaque bags	**Unit 3** week 6
Painting utensils	**Unit 2** week 4
Paper and pens	**Unit 1** weeks 1, 2
Photographs of children at different times of the day	**Unit 5** week 9
Pictures of butterflies	**Unit 1** week 2
Pictures of natural treasures (leaves, shells)	**Unit 4** week 8
Pictures of towers made from blocks	**Unit 4** weeks 7, 8
Pictures or photographs of analogue clock faces	**Unit 5** week 9
Plastic toy food	**Unit 1** week 3
Playdough or cake ingredients and recipe	**Unit 1** week 3 **Unit 5** week 9
Representations of numbers 1–5	**Unit 1** week 1 (1–3) **Unit 1** week 2 (1–4) **Unit 3** week 5 (1–5) **Unit 4** weeks 7, 8 (1–5)
Role-play toys	**Unit 1** week 2
Sand timer or stopwatch	**Unit 5** week 9
Selection of classroom items, small toys and real-life natural objects for counting and sorting, e.g. cars, animals, glue sticks, pens, leaves, conkers, shells , buttons, toy farmyard animals	**Unit 1** weeks 1, 2 **Unit 2** week 4 **Unit 3** week 5 **Unit 4** weeks 7, 8
Skipping rope or string	**Unit 1** week 3
Small objects for collecting	**Unit 3** week 6
Stories about times of the day and nocturnal animals	**Unit 5** week 9
Teaching clock	**Unit 5** week 9
Teddies	**Unit 1** week 3
Washing line, pegs and socks	**Unit 4** weeks 7, 8
Washing up bowl	**Unit 2** week 4
Wooden skewers	**Unit 3** week 6

Published by Pearson Education Limited, 80 Strand, London, WC2R 0RL.

www.pearsonschools.co.uk

Text and design © Pearson Education Limited 2019
Edited by Pearson and Just Content Ltd
Design templates created by Kamae Design
Typeset by PDQ Digital Media Solutions Ltd.
Original illustrations © Pearson Education Limited 2019
Illustrated by Andrew Painter and Nadene Naude at Beehive Illustration.
Cover design by Pearson Education Ltd
Back cover illustration by Andrew Painter
Cover illustration © Pearson Education Ltd 2019
Cover illustration by Andrew Painter

Power Maths Series Editor and *Power Maths Reception* Consultant: Tony Staneff

Written by White Rose Maths (Beth Smith, Amy How, Jane Brown and Faye Hirst), Beth Smith, Katie Williams, Faye Hirst and Caroline Hamilton.

First published 2019

23 22 21 20 19
10 9 8 7 6 5 4 3 2 1

British Library Cataloguing in Publication Data
A catalogue record for this book is available from the British Library

ISBN 978 1 292 28611 2

Copyright notice
Pearson Education Ltd 2019

All rights reserved. The material in this publication is copyright. The photocopiable sheets at the back of the book may be freely photocopied for classroom use in the purchasing institution. However, this material is copyright and under no circumstances may copies be offered for sale. No other part of this publication may be reproduced in any form or by any means (including photocopying or storing it in any medium by electronic means and whether or not transiently or incidentally to some other use of this publication) without the written permission of the copyright owner, except in accordance with the provisions of the Copyright, Designs and Patents Act 1988 or under the terms of a licence issued by the Copyright Licensing Agency, Barnards Inn, 86 Fetter Lane, London EC4A 1EN(www.cla.co.uk). Applications for the copyright owner's written permission should be addressed to the publisher.

Printed in the UK by Ashford Press Ltd

www.activelearnprimary.co.uk

The publisher acknowledges the use of the following material:
Photographs
123RF: Stockbroker, Unit 1. **Pearson Education**: Jules Selmes, Unit 4. **Shutterstock**: Zheltyshev, Antpkr, Ruth Black, Lorelyn Medina, Unit 1, Blend Images, Artjazz, Nick Jay Unit 3.

Note from the publisher
Pearson has robust editorial processes, including answer and fact checks, to ensure the accuracy of the content in this publication, and every effort is made to ensure this publication is free of errors. We are, however, only human, and occasionally errors do occur. Pearson is not liable for any misunderstandings that arise as a result of errors in this publication, but it is our priority to ensure that the content is accurate. If you spot an error, please do contact us at resourcescorrections@pearson.com so we can make sure it is corrected.